PHANTOM LIMB

PHANTOM LIMB

❧

THERESA KISHKAN

thistledown press

Library and Archives Canada Cataloguing in Publication

Kishkan, Theresa, 1955-
Phantom limb / Theresa Kishkan.

ISBN 978-1-897235-31-7
I. Title.

PS8571.I75P43 2007   C814'.54   C2007-904531-6

Cover photograph by Jan Westendorp@, all rights reserved
Cover and book design by Jackie Forrie
Printed and bound in Canada

Thistledown Press Ltd.
633 Main Street
Saskatoon, Saskatchewan, S7H 0J8
www.thistledownpress.com

| Canada Council for the Arts | Conseil des Arts du Canada | | Canadian Heritage | Patrimoine canadien |

Thistledown Press gratefully acknowledges the financial assistance of the Canada Council for the Arts, the Saskatchewan Arts Board, and the Government of Canada through the Book Publishing Industry Development Program for its publishing program.

Phantom Limb

❧

∽

Some say that an army of horse; others say that an army of foot soldiers;

Still others say that an army of ships against the dark earth is the most beautiful thing.

But I know it is what you love.

— Sappho (translated by Angelica Pass)

∽

Contents

Autumn Coho in Haskins Creek

I LIVE WITH my family in a temperate rainforest near Sakinaw Lake, which was once an inlet on the ragged coastline of British Columbia's great Inside Passage. Now the lake is separated from Georgia Strait by a swampy area created by decades of siltation; cliffs rise up from one side and on the other is a swift creek with a fishway leading from the lake into a small bay. We live at the far end of the lake, five or six miles from Georgia Strait.

When we first moved here, in the early eighties, we'd watch sockeye salmon gather and spawn in the gravel about six feet from the lakeshore at our end, their crimson bodies vivid in the clear water. Their carcasses would wash into the reeds, some of them pulled to shore by animals. We'd find a backbone, or a remnant of tail, in the tall grass. It's been several years since we've seen many sockeye at all and in fact this particular strain, the Sakinaw sockeye, notable for distinctive characteristics which mark them as genetically unique, has recently been declared an endangered species.

In those early days we didn't know there was also a coho run in nearby Haskins Creek although occasionally we'd caught

them while trolling for trout in the lake. Coho are another of
the five species of Pacific salmon. They are distributed widely
up and down the west coast but they represent only around
ten percent of the commercial salmon fishery. We knew they
spawned in other creeks feeding into the lake and in nearby
Anderson Creek. In some ways our lives were framed by fish,
not in the dramatic way the lives of the fishing families were,
but we began to expect our call in early summer to choose a
halibut to butcher for the freezer, and again in August to collect
our winter's supply of sockeye from a friend who fished out of
Prince Rupert. In late September we began to watch a nearby
creek for the cutthroat trout who swam in from another lake
to spawn. Trout brought kingfishers and heron to the bridge
over the creek and on lucky walks, we'd see them or hear the
kingfisher's dry rattle as it flew up from the water. We'd find
patches of chanterelle mushrooms to bring home for the table.
October rains filled Anderson and Meyer Creeks; the dark green
and red coho and the blotchy purple and pink chum salmon
that had gathered in Oyster Bay would begin the swim up to the
spawning beds and bears would gather to feast on the bodies.
Oysters were plentiful in autumn, too, either gathered from
remote beaches or purchased from commercial growers; and
some of the local fishermen set prawn traps, selling their catch
from the local dock. All winter we'd eat fish soups and slabs
of halibut grilled in the oven and sockeye barbequed outside
in the rain. In early spring we'd take our little boat out to the
lakes to drift the perimeters and troll for cutthroat. Sometimes
a friend would bring a side of smoked salmon or black cod
and we'd savour each sweet morsel. I'd want to know where
the fish had come from and we'd study the charts; I loved the

names of the fishing grounds — black cod from the San Juan Trench, sockeye from the Skeena runs. The fishermen would leave for the herring fishery and come home in a good year with money for vacations and new trucks. In summer there'd be the occasional fresh coho or spring salmon. You could see the wisdom in the traditional calendar of the Sechelt native people whose year was organized to reflect the cycles of cod eggs (March, the month of the black cod laying), coho and humpbacks entering the creeks (September and November, the months of the spawning), the ripening of berries (June, the month of salmonberries), the abundance of smoked salmon in the depths of winter (December, the month when the smoked salmon shed its skin).

In recent years the west coast fishery has entered a period of uncertainty. I have friends who are environmentalists and I listen to them catalogue the overfishing, the demise of runs, the destruction of particular habitats; and I have friends who are fishermen and I listen to them present a different picture, one complicated with regulations and restrictions, unfriendly neighbours, prohibitive expenses. I don't think there is a clear answer to any of the problems. What I've seen over the years in my own small habitat gives me room for joy and despair — the sight of a score of brilliant sockeye gathering in the shallow water where I walk, and six months later a score of power-boats, water-skiers in tow, churning up the gravel so necessary to egg incubation.

On the day of the winter solstice in 1997, weary of the debate surrounding the salmon conservation issues, we walked to Haskins Creek to see the coho. It had been a dark autumn for me as I accustomed myself to the absence of my oldest child who had left to attend Lester B. Pearson College of the Pacific, where kids gathered from all over the world to study together. The fish were a comfort, a parable of leaving and returning. When Forrest came back for the Christmas vacation, he brought a classmate, Youssef, a Palestinian boy from Lebanon, with him. We all walked to the creek to show Youssef something he'd never seen before in his mountain village. He was moved by the size of the fish in the narrow stream, and their absorption in finding the right place for the redds, the areas of creek bottom where the female prepares her nest sites in the gravel. We watched as the fish dislodged the gravel where it accumulated upstream, poised to wash down in the current to cover the fertilized eggs in their nests. It struck me as a metaphor for a young man who could not hold a passport, who had a travel permit with "Stateless" stamped on it like a bitter tattoo, and who would probably never return to that village in Lebanon.

This year we've been watching the coho in Haskins Creek since early November. It had been a hot dry summer and right into early October I wondered if there'd be enough water for the fish. The creek, overhung by broadleaf maples and salmonberry bushes, was very shallow, some of the gravel beds dry. But in mid-autumn, the rains arrived. Just as all the leaves had fallen, covering the ground with broad splashes of Naples yellow and ochre, the coho began to school in the bay by the mouth of Haskins Creek. There were common mergansers, the males with glossy green heads and the females with their rusty crests, swimming among the reeds which sheltered the gathering fish, and where the mergansers knew there would soon be fish-eggs washing down in the freshets. Several times a week we walk to the lake with our dog, enjoying the quiet now that the summer people have gone back to Vancouver for the winter, taking their big boats with them. Looking out over the calm surface, we see a sudden flash of silver as an eager fish, probably a jack, leaps from the water, leaving a widening circle of ripples. My son's return to college has been easier for me this year; knowing he'll be home for Christmas eased my sense of regret at the loss of what was: the pattern of our family in my daily life. Although our lives change, loved ones die — several good friends, a neighbour, and even one of the dogs who watched the fish with us last year died in the spring, her body now buried under old cedars in our woods — we need the constancy of place to anchor ourselves like a small boat in wild waters.

It's December and daily now, for nearly a month, coho have entered the creek in good shape, their bodies not yet tattered and bruised by their journey, or discoloured by the fungus that appears in their final days. They've made their way up to the gravel beds where the females nose the gravel to find the best place to excavate the redds. Males lurk in the vicinity while the females prepare their nests. Side by side you can tell the males from the females, their colour bolder, darker green and burgundy, and their jaws are hooked, mouths open. The water in Haskins Creek is very cold and clean, coming down off Mount Hallowell through deep forests, smelling of granite and moss. You can hear ravens klooking in the woods. Pairing up, the salmon spawn as they have done for thousands of years, laying eggs, depositing sperm, currents helping the silt to cover the eggs and lodge them in the gravel. There are so many coho this year that some of the fish are digging in areas claimed earlier by others; established redds are disturbed and the eggs scattered in the water to be eaten by birds and waiting cutthroat at the creek's mouth. We hear that dry rattle of kingfishers, the thin cry of eagles. Each time I walk the creek, I am moved to tears by the beauty of the fish, their bodies idling in the fast water or else pushing upstream over rocks and logs. There is radiance in their colour and shape, purpose in their movements; this culmination of a journey from as far away as the north Pacific to this small waterway, is proof that home — its scent and texture — has a place in deep memory. I hope there will still be a few pairs for Forrest to see when he arrives for the holiday.

Mid-winter is the season of miracles — children returning from distant enterprises; the chilly notes of old carols in the air; ancient stories of birth and death; two dark red fish sidling together in a riffle overhung with ferns, fish who have come such a vast distance through rain and under stars to find this unlikely water; a few loose eggs in the gravel glistening like a rare and costly gift.

∾

An Autobiography of Stars

WE HAVE ALWAYS made time in August to watch the Perseid meteor showers which appear so reliably. The Earth moves through the Perseid cloud as it stretches along the orbit of the comet Swift-Tuttle, and when Perseus rises in the northeast sky, the meteors fall from a point in that constellation. We often take guests to our second-storey deck where we lie back on the cedar boards, glasses of wine at hand, and watch the streaks of light across the heavens. But until autumn of 2001 I'd never seen the Leonid showers. They occur in November as the Earth crosses the orbit of the comet Tempel-Tuttle, the parent comet of the Leonid showers, between the 17th and 18th. Having heard that the show would be particularly rich that year, we set our alarm for the small hours of the morning and put out the chairs in readiness. My daughter asked us to wake her.

A child learns early to wish on stars. What dreams we attach to them, their silvery print on the dark cloth of the sky! I wished for fortune, for a horse, for someone to love me, for pain to vanish, for beauty. All of it came true, in time. When the Leonid showers washed our sky, the shooting stars were too swift and various to wish on, but what would there be now, in any case, for a woman to want in the richness of her middle years? I have written a book, planted a tree, loved and been loved by a man who continues to sleep at my side, built a house, and given birth to three children. And yet there are wishes, and wishes.

I am making a quilt of stars for my daughter. She is sixteen and has asked for a bed cover to replace the pink and green cats and hearts of her childhood. What colours now, I asked, and she suggested blues and purples. The bolts of cloth were almost too beautiful to choose from but there was an indigo like the night sky, there was a marbled cotton in deep blue and purple, and a soft silvery periwinkle like the starry flowers on the ground beneath our arbutus tree. I measured and cut, using my son's knowledge of mathematics for one difficult triangle, and pieced together stars of periwinkle and mauve to shine on a bed of dark blues.

When I was a child, I dreamed of beauty. What did it mean? I never knew exactly but was speechless with it sometimes, coming in from the fields with tears in my eyes, filled with something I had no words for. I was the odd one out at the table, amid the talk of hockey and hunting. Where did the sight of frog spawn on the rushes in the shallow end of a pool fit? Or the skeins of geese flying south overhead on golden fall days? I felt I would burst with the wonder of things and cried into my hands, inconsolable. Out of the blue, I found I could write poetry, a gift which allowed me to explore the mysteries of the world, but not understood by my family. It pained me to try to write in the shadow of anger and aggression I often felt in our household, filled as it was with unruly adolescents constantly at odds with their parents. Later, when I had a horse, I would press my face into his warm neck and murmur words that might have been poetry, might have been love. On his forehead, a white star against the black of his coat.

Is a parent ever aware of the brilliance of its offspring, a comet its shooting stars? Who can see such things clearly? Daily I remind myself to try. My sons, with their fine minds, intent on disciplines which will take them far out into the world, their lives trajectories beyond my seeing. My daughter is so lovely at sixteen, her blonde hair framing her face, her shapely blue eyes, that I am surprised each time she enters a room. Her intelligence startles me with its depth and maturity. My parents were of a generation reluctant to praise. I wonder if it had to do with religion, the fear that God might take away what was remarkable. I remember bringing home report cards with good grades but the questions would come: why a B? who got an A? And a comment on the report indicating a problem with attitude or effort would be seized and worked like a bone. I remember walking home from school with the brown envelope containing the report card in my satchel, anxiety causing my heart to flutter. I wanted to please my family but the things I excelled at were as foreign to them as Timbuktu: poetry, the explication of novels, classification of plants . . .

In thinking about meteors, the birth and passing of beauty, I look for books to tell me about astronomy. A few are very dry, cover photos showing author with impressive telescope, author adjusting lenses, author looking seriously into the sky with the naked eye. But one intrigues me, *Teach Yourself Astronomy*, by David S. Evans, from a series published in England in the fifties, the decade of my birth. It includes such titles as *Teach Yourself Anatomy*, *Teach Yourself Seamanship* and (my favourite) *Teach*

Yourself to Fly. I immediately went to the index to see if there was information on the Leonid Showers — there wasn't — but found the Appendices, a wonderful little collection of material: "The Greek Alphabet", "The Constellations", "Some Bright Stars", "A Short Astronomical Dictionary", and "A Book List", (annotated), directing the interested reader to books on telescope making, journals, as well as "An Important Reference Book (rather advanced)" called *Astrophysical Quantities.*

The "Short Astronomical Dictionary" defines a meteor this way: "small body rendered momentarily luminous by friction on entering atmosphere of earth." And meteor shower is "a group of meteors sharing common motion producing a display of numerous, almost simultaneous meteors." I read these again and am struck by how applicable the first definition is to a newborn child and the second to its family. I was recently given a copy of the telegram announcing my birth — my father was in the navy and was away at the time — and was moved to see myself described as "darling Theresa." I am certain I must have been praised as a child but the terms of possible endearment are lost to me in the tangle of hurt and absence that was my adolescence. I believed no one could love me.

A quilt takes months. You choose a pattern, something formal or an idea to cobble together. You try to think how much fabric you will need, translating shapes into metres, or in my case, yards, which I then convert. The fabric shop will make your choices difficult, all the bolts arranged by colour and tone, each more lovely than the last, or next. You will choose too much fabric, or too little. Wash it and dry it so that later washings, once the quilt is finished and used, won't shrink your coverlet out of shape. Cut out fabric into required pieces — for years I used scissors and nothing ever quite fit, which meant I had to compensate by constantly adjusting or easing things together. Then I bought a heavy vinyl mat, covered with grids, and a rotary cutter, which makes things easier and more accurate. But still. Make the blocks or arrange your collage of likely colours, textures, sewing them together by hand or with a machine. Fit these together in an agreeable way, realizing as you do so that your skills have not improved with the measuring, cutting, sewing, despite the fact that you've been doing it for years. More than a decade. Nearly two. Sandwich the batting between your quilt top of pieced blocks and whatever you've chosen for the back of the quilt (I have taken to buying cotton sheets, often seconds, from remainder bins, keeping an eye out for likely colours, and stockpiling them). Baste together with big stitches in a thread you'd never be able to use for anything else (the fuchsia in a assortment package, or the turquoise . . .). Then you can quilt. Using a frame or a hoop, using templates or freehand patterns which you've drawn with quilting pencils designed to fade after use, make the tiny stitches which draw the layers together and create texture. Be prepared for pleasure as you sit and stitch, working from the centre out to prevent wrinkles. By now you will see what I am seeing as I stitch my daughter's quilt, something unexpected, pale stars glowing in a deep blue sky.

Even so, no matter that I love to stitch, that I pick up the quilt whenever I can, that I honestly take solace in this homely handwork, it still takes months. I marvel at those who can work faster. I love for instance the story of the mice who help the tailor of Gloucester finish the Lord Mayor's waistcoat, their tiny paws working the buttonholes with tiny stitches, creating a festive garden of roses and pansies, of poppies and cornflowers. My stitches are nothing like mice-sized, but we are all watching the starry quilt eagerly as it nears completion, a constellation of stars for a young woman to dream under.

I look in "A Short Astronomical Dictionary" to see if there is a term analogous to quilting or the search for a thread to draw the stars closer to my daily life. Nothing quite fits. But there are definitions in the Dictionary which make oblique reference to qualities inherent in motherhood, in quilting, in watching the skies as a part of living intensely in a time and place. *Phase*, for instance: "used to describe degree of illumination of moon, planet or satellite. Also in sense of fraction of period of an recurrent phenomenon which has elapsed, as for example, in connection with variable star . . . " The pattern I am using for my daughter's quilt is the Variable Star. Quilt names have their origins in the work place (Monkey Wrench, Chimney Sweep), in travel and migration (Delectable Mountains, Oregon Trail, Wandering Foot); they reflect the lives and hopes of their makers (Log Cabin, Wedding Ring, Friendship Album) and have deep allegorical values as well. Quilts were used as codes for those using the Underground Railroad: a Compass Rose on a fence rail could either warn or encourage, depending on its placement; stars would echo the constellations leading north. A Variable Star is named for the possibilities within its design. It is pieced in small units of squares and triangles and there are untold variations inherent in this, correspondences between the maker and her materials, the outside world, future generations. A poetry of texture and anecdote, a guide to migration and continuity.

The night I woke my daughter to watch the Leonid Showers was cold and not quite clear. Mist from the lakes in the valley below us obscured the near sky to some degree but gradually drifted and lifted to allow better visibility. We understood that we should face east and try to locate the constellation Leo. We had a chart and knew to find Ursa Major, then follow a line down to Regulus, a bright star at the foot of the sickle-shaped line of stars that forms the head of Leo. The hindquarters are a sort of wedge-shaped group of stars. The sickle is the western portion of Leo and that is the radiant point for the meteor showers. Sure enough, we watched bright streaks rushing through the darkness. It is hard to find words of my own for the sight. However, in his 1563 treatise on meteors, *A Goodly Gallerye*, William Fulke expounded upon shooting stars: "A flying, shooting or falling Starre, is when the exhalation being gathered as it were on a round heape, and yet not thoroughly compacted in the hyghest parts of the lowest region of the ayre, beynge kyndled, by the soden colde of the mydle region is beaten backe, and so appeareth as though a Starre should fall, or slyde from place to place." This endearing description is oddly at one with my sensation that the meteors passed like the breath of fire: a few lines from across the centuries tell my story, a tale of a woman watching the Leonids with a daughter as lovely as starlight in the "mydle" region of the planet.

In quilting, geometrics have traditionally imposed the formats, the patterns. Some women are able to perceive a pattern spatially. I think of nineteenth-century examples of Tumbling Blocks or Grandmother's Flower Garden and am envious of the makers' abilities to think this way, to plan a project with an understanding of both depth and perspective. In planning a quilt, my reaction to this ordered system has always been a reckless measuring which produces careless results. Over the Christmas holiday, intent on beginning the Variable Stars, I asked my younger son, a physics and math major, how one could accommodate for seam allowances in a particular shape; I'd always arrived at this by hit or miss. He spent time working out an equation which he tried to explain to me but seeing I was lost, he produced a template with the equation as his blueprint. How easily his mind grasped the dimensions of a star, how well he saw that it was a sum of its parts and how best to represent each discrete element: first in an abstract calculation, then on paper, then in clean cotton.

One thing that has always puzzled me when looking at books about stars is the relationship between the pattern of the star and its name. So much must be taken on faith. Orion, for instance, is a constellation appearing in the classical astronomer Ptolemy's list of forty-eight constellations. Orion's is an ancient story with endless variations. A constant is that he was a hunter, but the thread that leads him to the heavens is lost in myth. One version of his story has him pursuing the seven sisters of the Pleiades. Variants of the myth have Orion pursuing their mother. Some sources suggest that this story evolved to explain the proximity of the two constellations and not the reverse. But to look at diagrams of Orion, the two triangles joined by the famous three-star belt, one must take it on faith that this is a hunter, the two bright stars, one of them Betelgeuse, forming his shoulders, and two more, his knees. Diagrams show the bow, Orion's arm raised to shoot. These stars are more elusive.

Ursa Major, the Great Bear, looks nothing like a bear to me but more resembles its variants — the Plough and the Big Dipper.

And Pegasus, the winged horse of the autumn sky — well, try as I might, with a heart eager for horses, I cannot see the horse hanging below the Queen Cassiopeia. If wishes were horses (and assuming I could see it), this is a constellation I would bridle with the help of Athene to bring on the wellspring of the Muses which was created by Pegasus by stamping his hoof on Mount Helicon. But that assumes that one takes on faith the relationship of those particular stars when in fact some of the stars within the formation are hundreds of light-years away from one another and if we were in different areas of the Galaxy, we would see something very different, another set of overlaid transparencies. And we are not seeing what is actually there in the real time of stars, a concept quite beyond my grasp. Yet humans have essentially viewed the same heavens since the dawn of recorded time, although stars are constantly in motion, being born and dying, shrinking and altering. Some explode. Some appear unchanged for centuries while others, the variables, brighten and fade over periods ranging from a few hours to a few days. The charts which illustrate the light curves of variable stars remind me of quilting charts. What impresses me most about both is that their creators have minds which can relate the abstract to the actual, curved lines of a star's light, geometric angles to a tactile object of cotton. I think again of the Tumbling Blocks and wish for such visual and spatial dexterity.

Later, discussing this, my husband says, "It's because you look at quilts as terrains, not maps." And I think, Yes, of course — for me they are collections of textures, colours, tracks of stitching across plain and printed surfaces. Getting fabric to mimic something I have seen — tulips in a bed of forget-me-nots, yellow and red against clear blue; velvets and corduroys to echo the patterns of fields seen from the sky; and now these silvery mauve stars pricking an indigo heaven. Something in relief, representational but not a leap from geometry to image; rather from hillock to valley, plant to its root system, meteorite to its brief flaring moment in the atmosphere of earth.

And looking to the sky, I see the way light resonates in a darkness beyond my imagining. I stand at my window at bedtime for a glimpse of heaven and see the moon: sometimes a sickle, or a full aching globe dusky with mountains. A topography, then, a terrain. I try reading it for its ridges and canyons, then look over to the spaces between stars, the long wash of light of the Milky Way. It doesn't matter that I've never been able to see the swan in Cygnus or the horse in Pegasus. Astronomers might argue that an understanding of the Doppler Effect or Kepler's Laws is fundamental to a discussion of celestial bodies. A scientist friend insists that science determines the way we see phenomena whereas I would rather call this another form of description, like poetry or music. Science doesn't necessarily get us any closer to the fact that the stars have their own integrity, or selfhood, without us applying the laws of physics. At my window, I am watching something that moves me deeply, a calligraphy of light to define the darkness.

William Fulke wrote, "the places in whiche Meteors are caused, be either the ayre or the earth, in the aire be generated rayne, hayle, snow, dew, blasing starres, thonder, lightning etc. In the earth be welles, springs, earthquakes, metalls, mineralls, etc. made, and as it were in their mothers belly begotten and fashioned . . . " The remarkable springs forth in surprising ways and needs to be acknowledged and praised. And so we make poetry, stories, connect the stars with lines to make patterns to reflect our own secrets and fears, or hopes and auguries. Consulting charts on graph paper, we plot a garden, a residence, the light curves of stars, a bridge to arch over a river to take us across safely, a quilt to echo our journey, our friendships, a flight of geese seen and never forgotten, bordered with pine trees, a compass rose.

I think of early people huddled into their animal skins beside a smoking fire, reading the sky like a bedtime story. Across the heavens, those tales unfold, light stitched to light, a tracery of twins, compasses, crowns and scales, virgins, the long sagas of hunters and heroes. We have in us a deep need for stories, to make the abstract literal, to offer narratives to explain the unknown. This is what I do when I cut my squares, thread my needles with strong cotton. I have been reading and remembering, finding a shape for the hurt of my own youth, hoping to spare my children from fear and regret. On each bed, a patchwork, for warmth and for safe passage through the night. In the sky we might fashion a parallel life, a world mirroring the topography of our own lives, irregular and beautiful, geometry in service to love. Sewing stars for my daughter to sleep under, I am fashioning a metaphor for my love of her and a belief in her luminosity, a parable of meteors and radiance and faith.

∾

The One Currach Returning Alone

And thereupon imagination and heart were driven
So wild that every casual thought of that and this
Vanished, and left but memories, that should be out of
season
With the hot blood of youth, of love crossed long ago . . .

— W.B.Yeats

I LIVED IN Ireland for nearly a year when I was in my early twenties. I arrived in April, coming by boat-train from London to Dun Laoghaire in the rain, then catching a bus to Dublin proper. I knew no one, and had no idea where I'd stay. But I had the reckless courage of the young, and sat by the window, watching the grey row houses with their lovely Georgian fanlights aglow in the smudged light of the traffic. A man sat beside me on the bus, and spoke in the accents of the Erin exactly as I had imagined, fresh from my Irish literature course; he told me he was a musician and that was that. He took me around to meet his friends, bought me my first pint of true untravelled Guinness, installed me in a raffish hotel with a good bar frequented by the music crowd, and got me a ticket for a Chieftains gig. I never saw him again. I spent three days in Dublin wandering the narrow streets, Georgian slums, and dark pubs where I somehow expected to see the characters of Joyce, Behan, O'Casey going about their business or stopping for a drink in a haunted corner at Davey Byrnes' establishment.

Someone at home, a printer and a film-maker, knew an old woman living in County Mayo. He'd gone to Ireland a few years earlier to make a film on the Troubles and had met Sheila because of her family connection to several heroes of the Easter Rising. If anyone can find you a place to live, it'll be her, he had said. I hitchhiked to Mayo in less than a day, across the middle of Ireland, lush farmland giving way to the rocks and Bens of the West. My heart leapt to the sight of stone walls and ruined cottages, camps of tinkers on the outskirts of towns. This was what I wanted and never had in the country I came from: the purity of low hills and hedges of fuchsia, men whose voices caressed my name and whose religion excluded me.

Sheila lived in a small caravan — she called it the Ark — in a corner of a stony field in rural Mayo. You ask to be let off at the round tower, I had been told in the letter she'd written to me that winter, and rounding the corner on a bus from Castlebar to Turlough, I suddenly saw it, grey and potent in its ancient churchyard where it had stood since the ninth century. Next to the churchyard, I sidestepped cow pats to reach her door. Smoke from a sweet turf fire bloomed from a chimney jutting crookedly out of the top of the caravan. Cats everywhere, concerned hens, a donkey. There was tea to drink and a narrow shelf to sleep on while she pondered where to send me. A friend in Louisbourg? The painters in Kerry? After a few days I realized I could easily listen to her stories forever and never leave the caravan at all so I set out on my own one morning in the rain for Galway and was sent by a fish dealer to a small island off the Connemara coast. I wanted to believe it was no accident — the house I rented, the fisherman who loved me, the blue and white teapot: I had waited all my life for them.

Each day, rain or shine, I climbed down the rocks to the sea. Sometimes I swam, or collected mussels for my dinner. Phlox surrounded my porch. I had a typewriter on a little wooden table in the scullery (the only room with good natural light and there was no electricity) and I wrote a book of poems. The men went out in precarious boats to drop lobster pots into the sea. The women knitted and gossiped. The islanders were the first generation of their community to speak English and they retained the Gaelic syntax. The past was spoken of in the present tense and history lived in each hour of the day. Everyone hated Cromwell and the rest of the English who'd sent them to the island in the first place; they repeated Cromwell's rallying cry *To Connaught or Hell* as though it had been uttered by a pesky politician that week and not three hundred-odd years earlier. When I said I was a poet, they asked Did I know the poet on the Arans. Which one, I asked. Ah, the one who wrote *Playboy of the Western World*, had I heard of that play? I had.

Two old bachelors, brothers, were my neighbours. They let me use their well and they gave me potatoes. At night they argued because one brother had given me turf and the other was jealous. I was the only unmarried woman they knew and I was courted with fuel and banty eggs, a pretty red fish called a gunnerd, trashy novels pulled out of a suitcase kept under a bed and smelling of mildew, jugs of buttercup-flavoured milk for my tea. One brother had no teeth, the other had a glass eye. Sometimes I wish I'd married one or the other just to have lived in their smoky cave where chickens pecked crumbs underneath the table and the Virgin Mary cried gilt tears above the mantle.

A man on the island played a tin-whistle most evenings on the boreen that led to the quay. If the wind was right, the notes would enter my cottage and coax me out to stand with a few others, in the lee of a hedge, listening as he played a few bars of this, a phrase of that, one or two trembling airs in their entirety. Occasionally I'd take my recorder out and we'd play together, usually *The Raggle Taggle Gypsies* because that was the only one I could play quickly enough to keep up. I bought a tin-whistle at a news-agent's shop in the nearby town, hoping that Miceal could teach me the fingering, but he'd get impatient with me and would take it and play some complicated jig that I couldn't begin to decipher, handing the whistle back to me, glazed with spittle.

A family had been raised in the cottage I lived in, six children living there with their parents until the mother's mother died and left them another house, slightly larger, which came with a job; it was the house that had always been the post-office and no one would dream of changing that. Only one of the six children remained with his parents, the others marrying and moving away, several to America, and one becoming a police officer or Garda in a village on the other side of the county. That son would come home most weekends with his wife and small child, carrier bags bulging with jugs of illicit poteen he'd confiscated from moonshiners in his village during the week. His parents often hosted ceilis on Friday nights to celebrate his visits and everyone got blind-drunk on the poteen, stumbling away in the small hours, singing sad songs at the top of their lungs in rain. I'd lie in my bed, listening, until the last one found his way home. Occasionally one or two of the unmarried men would stand above my cottage and sing until their voices gave out. In daylight these were men who would pass me on the boreen, faces scarlet, too shy to say hello.

What did I want there, what did I find? I learned something of lobsters, where they lurk in the cold Atlantic, something of isolation in my north-facing cottage. I was the only person living on the island who did not attend Mass. When I explained that I'd been raised by a Presbyterian mother and a lapsed Catholic father, I saw eyebrows raise and significant looks being exchanged. It was as though I'd told them my parents had never been married.

I'd come from a painful love affair and wanted to forget about men. But everywhere were those soft voices, the smell of peat and tweed and sweat. I could no more say no to the shy fisherman who visited me with his aging dog than I could say no to the dawn trips in the currach to set nets or look at the seals on the rocks to the west of the island. He'd come at night, bringing a handful of parsley from his father's garden or a pot of his mother's marmalade. I'd make some tea for us and we'd sit by my fire until the candles burned down to nothing. It took him ages to unlace his boots and he was beautiful in moonlight. I'd wake in the morning to find him gone and only the sweet peaty smell of his hair on the pillow next to mine. When I fished with him, he'd stay longer, waking first to make strong tea for me to drink while he brought his currach around to my beach. We'd head out just as the sun came up beyond the Bens of Connemara and come back late, cold and wet, with a box of lobsters clattering under damp burlap or a string of mackerel. He'd drop me in front of my cottage and I'd make myself some soup, drinking it quickly before falling asleep to the smell of the North Atlantic coming in through my curtains.

I remember how lovely the hills were in autumn, the russet and gold of the furzes, and how the wind smelled of sheep. My house was cold. The windows all rattled and wind came right under the doors until I put newspapers in the cracks to hold it back. Why someone had built it in its north-facing location was beyond me. It stood on a promontory and I felt as though we'd be lifted up in the fierce November gales, the house and I, to be taken far out to sea on the wind. And I wondered if anyone would miss me. The fisherman had begun to come less often, preferring his mother's warm kitchen with its big chairs and pot of mutton stew. He knew, even if I didn't want to, that there wasn't a future in our sort of union. His own uncle had married a woman from an island half a mile to the north and had moved there to live in a house she'd been left. This man was considered a "blow-in" by the other islanders and his children were isolated as a result. The uncle told me once, at a cattle fair in the mainland town where we all did our shopping, that he'd look from his house at night to see the soft gaslights of our island and wish to God he'd never left.

When I decided to leave, people came to my house to tell me they were sorry I was going. They brought little gifts — cards, a loaf of soda bread, a toque of Connemara wool which blew off my head during the ride across to the mainland and couldn't be retrieved with an oar. My fisherman rowed me across with my rucksack and shook my hand formally, wishing me safe passage home. I walked up to the road, wondering how soon a ride would come; my pack was heavy and the seven miles to the town was a long walk. When I turned to look at the island, it was as though it had never known me, hunched under the wind with a few wisps of smoke rising and the one currach returning alone.

Back in Dublin again I stayed in the same raffish hotel just long enough to give a few poetry readings arranged by a friend and attend a play or two. I bought books to take home and a record of Paddy Tunney singing *Donal Og*. When I walked along Grafton Street or through Stephen's Green, it was as though I was dreaming. I wanted to wake to my cold room and the smell of peat, wanted to wake from the decision to leave and find myself still wrapped in the fisherman's arms or else climbing into his boat while a few terns mewed in the wind above us. From this distance, across the width of Ireland, the problems of background, isolation, religion seemed easily solved. But I remember boarding the plane with a weight that settled down through my throat into my heart and was so heavy I thought I could never walk with it, or be able to talk. This is so long ago now but thinking of it brings back the music of Miceal's tin-whistle as clear as anything and I ache to walk out to the boreen and learn to play along.

∽

COLTSFOOT

EVERY YEAR, IN early April, I am surprised all over again at the sight of coltsfoot blooming on the side of the highway near my home on the Sechelt Peninsula. This is *Petasites palmatus*, sweet coltsfoot, a beautiful broad-leafed plant with umbels of white or pink-tinged flowers. I'm surprised because the trees are still quite bare, the alders and maples, though the leaves are beginning to unloose themselves from the tight furls on the branches. Underneath the maples, the small clusters of chartreuse blooms have fallen, lying on the ground, insects climbing over them for their honeyed taste. I anticipate the maples in April. But it is startling to suddenly see the lush coltsfoot filling the ditches, scented like celery, flowers foaming over the verdant leaves. Every year I forget. And then am surprised.

Almost forty years ago, I was a girl with a horse. He was an Anglo-Arab colt, not quite three years old. His coat was black, he had three white socks, and a blaze on his handsome face. I loved him with all the ardour that a teenaged girl has to offer. I'd kiss his soft muzzle over and over, murmuring endearments. I did not yet ride him. He came to me accustomed only to the halter and lunge line. He was ready to be trained as a saddle horse and I was going to do it.

My father built a small stable for him. Well, it was a shed, made of plywood and two-by-fours, a rail inside separating my horse's stall from the area where I kept some bales of hay, a sack of feed, and my small supply of grooming equipment: a curry comb, some rags, a hoofpick, a dandy brush, the softer body brush. He had a blue webbing halter and a lead to match. I loved to snap the lead to the ring on his halter and walk him around the farm we lived on — we didn't own it or even work it ourselves; we rented the old farm house which the two brothers who owned the farm deserted in favour of modern bungalows they'd built next door. The brothers graciously allowed me to keep my horse in the orchard paddock next to our house. Sometimes I walked him as far as the creek where I'd let him graze on the rich grass while I sat and watched for frogs. Sometimes I'd take him along Townshipline Road to get him used to traffic. He shied a little at first when a car passed but eventually stopped showing any kind of concern, apart from a long ripple of the muscle that ran up his neck from his strong shoulders.

I sang to my horse. While I curried him, brushed him all over with the dandy brush, combed the tangles out of his mane, and polished him with the soft cloth, I crooned all the songs that I'd begun to really listen to in my fourteenth year. They were songs of yearning and broken hearts. I hadn't listened much to popular music before that but had sung in a school choir and earlier, a church choir in the days when my family still attended. My father had been transferred when I was thirteen, and we moved to the farm the summer before I entered grade

eight. Everything changed. No more knee socks and pony-tails.
Girls wore some sort of garter belt and sheer stockings; they
shaved their legs (it never occurred to me to do this until I was
sitting in school assembly with my class and noticed the legs
of the girls around me were all smooth whereas mine had dark
hairs flattened against my stockings); they applied Maybelline
mascara onto their eyelashes with a brush and a little red box of
hard pigment that had to be dampened first. Pale pink lipstick.
Short skirts — it was 1968. I'd go to school in my panty girdle
and short skirt (often rolled shorter once I'd left the house), my
hair teased on top, my purse full of Tangee lipsticks and black
mascara. At school there was the confusing theatre of dating
to figure out, how one would dance with a boy at the noon-
hour sockhops (if it was a slow dance, did you put your arms
around the boy's neck or his waist? Did it matter?). There were
magazines — *Seventeen* and *Teen Beat* — which gave advice on
kissing or body odour.

And there wasn't a school choir. Or maybe there was but I
couldn't have stayed after school for practice because our bus
left about ten minutes after dismissal and I had no other way
home. I missed the work of trying to hold my own notes in
a madrigal while all around me others sang their own parts,
our voices eventually braiding and blending in harmony. But I
found something in pop music on the radio. I thought it had a
message for me although I couldn't have said what, exactly.

Once I was offered a ride with a grade ten boy named Bob
Schroeder whose farm wasn't far from where we lived, and who
rode a motorcycle to school. I had a crush on him and happily
accepted the ride, my arms wrapped around him from behind.
He stopped on the way back, in a remote area off the main road,

and began to kiss me. I'd never been kissed by a boy before and didn't know what to do. His tongue at my mouth seemed odd and a little repulsive. But it was also insistent and eventually my own mouth softened, opened.

After he'd dropped me at my house, I went in, mouth swollen with his kisses, and was immediately grounded for a month. My crime? Accepting a date when I wasn't yet allowed to date. I hadn't known I wasn't allowed. The topic had never come up. At my elementary school, I wasn't at all popular with the boys I'd known for years. I was taller than them for one. I matured early and I suppose my breasts must have terrified them. But at this new school, in this new community, no one had known me as a very gangly pre-adolescent. I was a girl with a womanly figure and no history. Fair game. I didn't know this at first but soon noticed there were boys hanging around my locker, older boys asking their younger sisters who the new girl was. My brothers had friends who seemed interested.

The kissing dilemma — open mouth and tongue — was soon resolved by reading a reply in an advice column in one of the teen magazines. I think every girl of my age was curious about kissing. Of course we practiced on our arms, particularly the soft skin of our inner arms, and in my case, on my horse. But one didn't have a chance to practice kissing French style until one had a partner of the opposite sex who was interested in the whole enterprise. I don't remember exactly what the columnist advised but in any case the next time kissing came up, I was prepared. What I began to understand, not that year perhaps but certainly not long after, was that the tongue was an early taste of what was to come. Odd and a little unsettling at first — something moist and urgent seeking to enter my body — but eventually a pleasure. The mouth anticipating what the vulva would eventually be eager to receive.

I loved to groom my black horse. And he loved me to do it. Starting at his neck, working down and along his body to his hindquarters, then moving to the other side. The near side, the far side. The final act was leaning against him, taking up each foot in my hand, carefully cleaning the hollow areas around the frog with the hoof pick, removing the compacted earth and manure. Sometimes when I cleaned his feet, my horse would turn his head and blow on the back of my neck. His breath smelled of sweet hay and the molasses which flavoured his feed.

It was astonishing to hold the foot of such a powerful animal in my hand. To cradle the foot, bent at the slender ankles with their tufts of hair at the fetlock, and to realize how the weight of a body could be supported by such a network of bone and sinew, the elastic substance of the inner foot, the ever-growing material of the hoof itself, like horn. I spent hours with him in the stable or his orchard. A girl longs for physical affection and my horse provided the warmth and close intimacy that was lacking in those early teenaged years. I didn't want my parents to hug me, nor did they often try. They were frequently angry with me for one reason or another (falling grades, moodiness), and this was the beginning of the long journey away from them. I'd close the door of my bedroom and listen to my radio or the small collection of 45s I'd begun to buy. Every part of my body felt strange and elated. I'd stand in the mirror and look at my waist, my breasts, the new tendrils of hair over my pubis. I'd imagine my hands to be the hands of some unlikely suitor. The magazines assured one that touching oneself was normal and healthy but in my room under the gable end of our old house, it felt a little shameful and wrong.

Songs would enter my head, fill me with anticipation and desire — Tommy James, the Beatles, the Union Gap, the Rolling Stones. The knowing language which spoke of the flame of passion, the agony of separation, the inevitability of betrayal — I couldn't wait for a relationship of my own which might inspire a song, a poem. I'd sing to my horse with all the longing of my years and he'd listen, his ears twitching a little. Sometimes I'd cry, wondering how long it would be before I had a love to call my own, dedication from the one I loved, a chance to be someone's earth angel, brown-eyed girl. These were songs that needed to be sung, not with the choir on its risers, sheet music in front of us, the performance public and formal, but alone, in a stable smelling of straw and warm grassy breath.

I wondered how I would break him, this large black colt with the beautiful dished face — his Arab inheritance — and the tail that flew behind him like a flag when he galloped from one end of his orchard to the other. How would I train him to the saddle and bridle, to respond to the pressure of my knees on his sides, my hands sending messages from the thin leather reins to his mouth that held the metal bit. I'd taken riding lessons for several years but had never mounted a horse that hadn't been trained to carry a rider around a ring or along a trail, mildly and dutifully. I'd intended to buy a horse like that. But having looked at a few, ridden them, and not having loved them, I was ready to be taken completely by the dark eyes and bold manner of this one. I lost my heart immediately on seeing him in the paddock of a breeding farm near Yarrow.

Books were helpful — to a point. Other people were helpful, too. But finally one day, after I'd accustomed my horse to the bridle I'd bought with babysitting money, I led him to the gate of his orchard and held the reins while I draped my body over his back like a sack of oats. He was interested but not troubled. He turned to look at me and then flicked his tail. I did the same thing a few more times without incident. And then I straddled him bare-back (I didn't yet own a saddle), holding my breath.

In later years, people stopped talking about breaking horses and referred to it as gentling them, schooling them. Nothing was broken in my early years with my horse apart from my pelvis, when I was fifteen and he reared as we were making our way up a hill in a windstorm — I was holding him in because I didn't want him racing up and shying at something blown in our path, as he had sometimes at a pheasant, or leaves, or even the tall grass itself. He reared, lost his balance, and fell back, landing in my lap as I hadn't been able to throw myself clear. I spent two months in the hospital, the first perfectly flat on my back to let the pelvic bone knit back together and the other in extensive rehabilitation to learn to walk again.

Nothing else was broken, nothing lost apart from my heart to that large animal with his exquisite smell and coat like rubbed silk. I know that horses are thought to be symbols of sexual drive and fertility, and I will say this is true. Straddling that warm animal, I was never more aware of the latent possibilities of my own body, the rich musculature that began and ended between my legs. No boy I ever kissed gave me that sense of my own power. To learn that in a small orchard, with a submissive horse whose flanks one has groomed, polished with a soft cloth, whose muzzle one has kissed and shared breath with, whose feet one has held, one by one, to clean and care for, was to partake of the most urgent of mysteries. What was awakened was also a gradual sense of knowledge — that my body was capable of strength and power. I was ready for the life ahead, leaving that room with its single bed and girlish things, to travel on my own, find my voice as a woman, a writer. I was preparing for passionate love with my husband, the passage of my children down through my body to enter the world.

I stop on the roadside and carefully lift a plant of the coltsfoot to bring home to my own garden. *Petasites palmatus*, butterbur, sweet coltsfoot. There are the blooms on their fleshy stalks and the broad leaves with fine hairs on the underside. And there is one small inrolled leaf-shoot, not yet opened, the foot of that colt I hold as I once held the entire weight of his delicate ankles in my hands.

∾

Shadows Over the Red Hills

WE LIVED IN Utah the winter of 1990, leaving our house on the Sechelt Peninsula three days after Christmas to drive down through Washington and across the great plains of Oregon and Idaho to a state we'd never seen. My husband had been invited to be a visiting writer, would teach classes of creative writing and give readings of his work; the university that had invited him was to provide us with housing for our stay.

We'd never lived away from home as a family, though my husband and I had both spent winters in other countries before we met — Greece, England, Italy, Ireland — and our children were keen to explore new ground. We looked forward to living in a town for a few months. Concerts, dinners out, long walks at night under streetlights: these held attractions for our family accustomed to a life centered around the home fire. Our nights were filled with owls and loons, our days held long drives for groceries and school but also the pleasures of an orchard and garden. We packed our warmest clothing, bought snow boots all around, made arrangements for our dog and cat, and caught an early ferry for the mainland.

I knew Eastern Washington, had explored its coulees and little towns as a younger woman, but hadn't expected the golden fields of Oregon, a sky that went on and on. Sunlight gilded the wings of hawks floating over the shorn plain and poured into our van. We bought dry salami, good bread, a bag of crisp apples and Tillamook cheddar in Pendleton, and picnicked on a hill that overlooked remnants of the wagon road leading to the Willamette Valley. There were pine trees, and I collected their huge cones to take back with us. How far we'd come, I mused, that we could eat on a cold hill with the world stretching out in all directions at the end of an old year.

I think we expected to find a charming old University town with ivy clad buildings and long avenues lined with ethnic restaurants, bookstores, something like Oxford, maybe, or Berkeley. Instead, we found Provo. There *was* a pretty part to the town with some old buildings and one Mexican restaurant but no one lived in that area, or wanted to. Anywhere else it would've been the town's heart but in Provo we came to see that people flocked to the malls and strip developments, endless fast-food places that served hamburgers, donuts, or fake tacos day and night. We drove up the main road, past the huge malls and McDonalds, and wondered what on earth we'd done.

At the University, we found someone to take us to where we were to live. In order to be allowed to rent an apartment on campus, we learned we had to sign a form saying we'd obey the laws of the church that sponsored the University: this meant no premarital sex, no beards, no adultery, no coffee. My husband was given a special letter of permission for his beard and we reasoned that our coffee habits were our own business. Our apartment was part of Family Housing, a huge complex tucked up behind the campus where many hundreds, maybe thousands, of families lived while the husbands attended classes. The women were discouraged from being anything but mothers, and during the day the sidewalks and laundry rooms were full of them with their small parades of children and baskets of wet clothing. There were classes advertised that would teach home decorating and soup-making.

After I'd asked why women were not allowed to have important roles in the church hierarchy, some of my neighbours visited to explain their position as mothers and nurturers of their husbands. They were nice women, good-humoured, but I was uncomfortable with their conviction that this what God wanted of them — and of me, too, as one of them assured me. He loved us, I was told, in His own way. We continued to meet occasionally but I felt that gap — of expectation, of faith, and of acceptance of what seemed to me an enormous lack of gender equity. It hung between us like a chasm.

Our furnished apartment in Family Housing resembled a Motel 6 or any of the cheap motel chains strewn along the Interstate highway system. Elderly unloved furniture, a bare minimum; a tiny functional bathroom, which discouraged lingering; institutional drapes on windows looking out onto the parking lot. I remember putting together the children's iron-framed beds, the paint chipped and the mattresses stained from years of use. We hung posters of marine life and poetry broadsheets and draped the drab standard lamps with gauzy shawls, circa 1972. In a way our lives became secretive, lived out behind the drapes in hushed voices which took practice: "Quiet, remember we have neighbours . . . "

We were not unhappy in Utah, though our lives seemed diminished. At home, we lived on a grassy bluff in a coastal forest, surrounded by gardens of our own making and then the woods taking off from the edges of our lawn. There were no close neighbours, though people lived in the area and could be counted on to help when necessary. Friends lived close as the crows fly but farther than expected when travelling by road. In the apartment, we could hear our neighbours make love on one side and quarrel on the other. Upstairs, children ran back and forth along an uncarpeted hall and when the smallest one learned to walk, we heard the heavy hesitant footsteps and then his cry when he fell. We heard televisions and laughing.

We did not live in nature as we do here. Our apartment lay at the foot of the mountains, a stone's throw, but to get to them we had to wade through the detritus of residents at odds with the landscape in which they found themselves: no wind-chimes, or gardens, apart from vegetable plot allotments come April; no compost heaps or weathervanes or areas where one could sit and look east to the Wasatch Mountains or due west to the vast desert stretching as far as California, with little runs of mountains in between. Instead, there were tricycles, basketball hoops, toys inspired by every television show possible (Ninja turtle swords, GI Joe dolls lying legless and stricken, Care Bears with the stuffing bashed out of them), and we found the spent shells of shotguns. Later, in April, the sad trees which children maimed at regular intervals, whacking at them with shovels or large sticks, bloomed with a vitality I would not have thought possible. My oldest son, equipped with binoculars, notebook and birthday camera, took notes and photos of the plants on the hills of scrub oak behind us. As the season progressed, he recorded the emergence of wildflowers — sego lilies, long-leaved phlox. One day he returned from his hills in tears because some older boys had taunted him, telling him that everything was put on earth for the use of man. They stepped on the lilies he'd been watching for weeks and called him a dirty Catholic. One of them took a BB gun and killed the pair of grouse my son had been following, hoping to see their nest. Mornings, that spring, I woke early to bird song and thought I was home until I oriented myself in the strange bed (*still*, after four months) — window there, yes, wall, closet — and then looked out to the back of 15A and one small flowering crabapple, limbs bare of robins but the lingering descendant note of their joy still echoing. A broken kite hung from that tree, fluttering in wind like a trapped bird, until the grounds crew removed it.

Our middle child woke in the nights during those months, weeping for home. Close your eyes, I'd say, and think about what your room at home looks like. Dream your way back into your bed and go to sleep now. It's always there for you and four months will go like anything. Lying under the worn brown blanket — the apartment came with bedding, clean but shabby — with his arms clutching his small teddy bear, he'd attempt to do as I suggested, and some nights it worked momentarily, but other nights, there'd be the same sound of crying from his room and I'd tell him the same charm: think of home.

I remember the freedom we felt when we realized that nothing was to be gained by staying in Provo on the weekends. That first experimental weekend, we planned a trip to southern Utah. I made food to take along so that we could get off the beaten track and eat where we pleased — a terrine of pork and beef, wrapped in bacon, to slice onto rye bread; baked chicken; trail mix of almonds, raisins, sweet dried apricots. We ate our first lunch on a hill looking out over Green River with the snowy LaSals far beyond. There were hawks and blue pinyon jays. That weekend stretched to five days because we didn't want it to end. We drove into Arches National Park mid-afternoon with Hadyn's cello concerto on the tapedeck. The air was intensely dry and pungent with sage and we walked around the enormous fins of red rock rising out of the desert, articulated here and there with great windows. Looking through them, you saw Colorado.

We'd never known anything like southern Utah. In the little town of Moab, near Arches, we ate huge steaks in a cowboy cafe that served wine and coffee. After Provo, this was decadence. We picnicked from our basket of food on a high promontory above the confluence of the Green and Colorado Rivers, a sight more spectacular to us than our later sighting of the Grand Canyon. Here, we were the only people standing high above the world, watching thin threads of water far below and the exquisite chasms of rock, red and ochre and striated with charcoal. On a small rocky ledge below where we stood on the Island in the Sky lookout, we saw, to our surprise, Douglas firs, a familiar enough tree to us but alien to this country of stunted juniper and yucca. Were they survivors of an earlier climatic period, were they seeded by wind or birds? Their growth was made possible by the constant seepage of water through the rock surrounding them but we saw them nowhere else in Utah. A tiny biotic zone, like a museum, there in a land populated by rattle-snakes and lizards.

There was wind that blew red sand into our faces, drying our mouths. Later, we drove along the Colorado River on a narrow road leading to a sulphur mine. The cliffs above the road were embellished with pictographs — lines of people holding hands, spiders, curly-horned sheep, suns, a graffiti left a thousand years ago, and there were bullet holes made by those coming later. Pieces of pipe, carefully mounted at strategic places along the river, were focussed like telescopes. We peered through them to see cliff dwellings in one place, the huge footprint of a three-toed dinosaur in another. Further along the highway, we stood on a trail in the dry air watching a small lizard sleeping amid the fossilized vertebrae of a sauropod.

Another weekend, we drove across Northern Arizona to the sound of wind, while we watched the sun and cloud make shadows run over the red hills among the sheep and thin ponies. We wanted to explore the Anasazi cliff villages, abandoned 800 years ago but still reasonably intact. We stayed in a motel near Kayenta, waking in the morning to new snow which made our first destination, Betatakin, a treacherous undertaking. We crept along the road at snail's pace, finally arriving at an information centre to discover we couldn't hike right to the ancient cliff dwelling as we'd hoped. What we *could* do was walk to a hill opposite Betatakin where a telescope was located. In a way it brought us closer than we could have dreamed. There, surrounded by the yucca, sharp and brittle, which the Anasazi people had used for sandals, and the willow they'd woven into baskets, we looked at that ancient abandoned settlement huddled under the side of a cliff. Once our eyes became accustomed to the slight distinctions in the colour of rock, depth of shadows, we could see the paths leading up from the valley bottom where crops had been carefully cultivated, making use of any run-off from the rare falls of rain. Ladders leaned against the pueblos, ready for someone returning from the gardens of corn and gourds. Our breath in the cold air, their smoke. I felt I was seeing evidence of a high point in human history where small groups of people had lived in a self-contained community, centering their lives around the family (small babies had been found buried near the fire pits, close to their mothers, tiny shoes alongside), making baskets of extraordinary beauty, a beauty found in the pottery of the later Anasazi, born of practicality, wasting nothing, making whistles of bird bones, rattles of deer hooves. I was deeply moved by their medicine bags when we saw them in the information centre's museum — corn pollen, beads of animal bones, small fertility figure of clay. I was spellbound, as though I might discover a way to take the meaning of these objects into my own life. To make offerings of seeds and the cleaned bones of sheep.

Coming back to the apartment always seemed anticlimactic. We'd park in front and unload our stuff — rocks, boughs of sage to fill the air of our rooms with earthy perfume, laundry of course — and fit ourselves into those rooms again after days in the desert. What amazed me was how little the people around us knew of the State. Where did you go this time, they would ask, and we would tell them — Moab or Zion or to see the eagles at Ophir (just two hours away). Or New Mexico or Arizona. Many of them skied so they knew the ski resorts in the mountains just at our backs but they didn't seem to need wilderness, or want it. The history that they spoke of involved an ancestor who'd come out with Brigham Young or an uncle who'd dry-farmed at Nephi. Dry farming involved the heavy use of herbicides over thousands of acres of grassland to kill everything but the grasses for hay. It would turn out that the uncle had actually lived in a town and drove out to the hayfields when they needed attention. Some lived on the farms, of course, but love of earth and the sky was never spoken about. Ancestors and current kin were taken to heart, worshipped, and genealogy was a subject that was discussed and examined at great length. The deep past, of the land and the Basket People and the dinosaurs, this seemed foreign to them, or unnecessary.

One Friday, without having planned to do anything in particular, we decided to leave immediately after the children were dismissed from school. A phone call to the weather office for the state revealed that the roads in and around the Dinosaur National Monument in the north-eastern part of Utah, where it met Wyoming and Colorado, were open (it was a cold week in March). We drove up over the Wasatch Range, passing snowplows enroute but then driving for miles through grasslands, wild and golden. We arrived at Vernal at dusk and found an Econolodge where we were given two rooms for the price of one, joined by a bathroom; this meant we wouldn't all be sleeping in the same room, a special treat on these trips! The next morning we headed out early to look at the extraordinary display at the Dinosaur National Monument. The visitor centre had been built over an excavated bank showing a large concentration of fossilized remains of dinosaurs, and prehistoric turtles; it was the bed of an ancient river in the midst of desert terrain. Scaffolding up and along the bank showed the work of paleontologists, who had been there as recently as the day before. Femurs were emerging from the washed rock, as well as rounded shapes that might be skulls, and even the hardened carapace of a turtle. From there we drove through the park, alerted by a brochure to an overhang where the Fremont people had made a winter camp, leaving bones and dried corn and medicine bags which were on display in the museum in Vernal. In another place, high on a sheer rock face glazed with desert varnish, the name given for the dark patina formed by minerals in clays distributed over canyon walls, we found pictographs of lizards climbing up towards the sun. Near them, behind a chunk of rock, the artist had carefully scraped away the patina to outline a hand in the red rock, and the littlest lizard of all. Further along, the trapezoid shape of a Fremont princess, barebreasted and sturdy, not unlike the Venus of Willendorf in her beauty. It was hard to take in all the messages coming across the centuries and millennia; our senses were numbed after awhile to their meanings. Later, I'd make notes in my journal and discover that I was describing what I'd seen in the language of the Psalms.

What I remember most about that trip to Dinosaur National Monument was the small abandoned ranch within its boundaries, settled by a woman, the brochure told us. I could tell that a woman had lived there by the remnants of flower beds — iris and lilac and cornflowers, not in bloom in March, of course, but the new growth of them emerging from under their covering of scrub oak leaves — and the sight of the old chimney wrapped in unpruned rampant growth of wild clematis. The ranch was nestled in at the bottom of the beginnings of mountains, at the edge of the desert; a creek, green with watercress, flowed through the area where the cabin had been built. There were box-canyons, squared on three sides by high rock and the remains of fences on the open ends. Seepage from the rock walls and hidden springs kept the box-canyons green and would have provided perfect, contained grazing for cattle and sheep. The few old cottonwoods would have offered shade to the stock. A strand of old rope hung from the high branches of one, testifying to the presence of children in those years. I couldn't help but imagine my family into that life, find room for them in the cabin, locate them in the work of the place. The small barn seemed so familiar and the hawks floating high on the thermals made me fear for imagined poultry. We come upon these places at times in our lives, feel drawn to them for reasons unknown except in the heart, and leave them again with a deep regret. Our sense of leaving home is no less for never having lived there.

We drove back to Provo by a long route through Wyoming, stopping at Fort Bridger to look at the settlement there and visit the museum. This was the country of legend, mountain men and big horses and huge skies. Everywhere you looked, you saw open space. The freeway signs announced Denver and Cheyenne, names as haunting as a country song, and the hills were punctuated with oil derricks on their wild slopes. The map sang its own poetry which we barely had time to listen to because we had to drive late into the night as it was — Sweetwater River, Thunder Basin National Grasslands, the Rattlesnake Hills. Coming back to Family Housing never seemed so sad.

Some mornings when my children were in school and my husband at the University, I'd drive out to the edge of town and try to orient myself by clouds and the mountains. To the northwest were the Great Salt Lake and the Lakeside Mountains where we'd climbed with friends and found a fossil bed of paleozoic corals and crinoids. To the far south was Monument Valley. East, right behind our apartment, the Wasatch Range of the Rocky Mountains and north of that, the Tetons and the Bitterroot Range. Clouds were high and rolling, like herds of buffalo, dust rising around their powerful bodies. I'd close my eyes and breathe in the intense odours of rabbitbrush and mesquite, the dry air rushing through my nostrils and down into my lungs with stinging clarity. When we'd first arrived, I thought this land was bare, beautiful in its simplicity. But after spending time looking at the ground at my feet, I'd begun to see the diversity of plant-forms and even the red earth itself revealed its shades and depths. The plants themselves were economical, grey leaves and hairy texture to preserve moisture, succulent stems, low-growing. Some armed themselves with spines or barbs, some stank so that animals would leave them alone. I began to feel at home out among the plants and the sky; the clamorous pinyon jays became nearly as dear and familiar as their cousins, the Steller's Jays of our coastal landscape — a bright wink of blue sailing from tree to tree in search of seeds. No matter that the trees here were scrub oak and juniper and not the lofty red cedars of home.

My middle child stopped weeping in the night and began to collect objects to remind him of our adventures. I made him a drawstring bag to store things in and it hung on the door to his room like a medicine bag: a small flake of petrified wood; juniper berries smelling of gin; a perfect tetracoral found on top of the Lakeside Mountains, unearthed from a long dream of the sea. Utah wasn't what we expected; the housing was too bleak; the culture was not our own; and we learned how bound we were to our ground on the Sechelt Peninsula and how the imprint of our feet meant something, or would, to the soil of our home. But there are ways of passing through the valleys and mountains of this world, eyes open to the colours and movement, nose alert to the wind, and ears tuned to the sound of those who have been and will come again.

∾

Laundry

THE ONLY ONE allowed to do laundry in my mother's house was my mother. The washing machine stood against one basement wall with a deep double sink between it and the dryer. There were lines of nylon string crisscrossing the basement, strung from the rafters above the wooden bins and shelves, the boxes of old hockey equipment, the drill press given to my father by his workmates as a retirement gift. A hand sewn canvas bag contained clothes pegs. The lines always held something — old rags, dishcloths, damp socks — but there was still room for at least a load or two of laundry to be pegged up to dry in the stale air of the basement. On fine days, my mother hung her wash outside and it came in smelling of the wind and sunlight.

There were strict rules about laundry. It had to be dirty. You couldn't put in a pair of jeans worn only once or twice unless you'd spilled something on them. Ditto for shirts. Wash was usually done on Mondays, a salute to the time, which I well remember, when a wringer washing machine was used and laundry was a day-long job. There were always sheets, of course, and a week's worth of underwear (you were expected to change your underwear daily in the event you were in an accident) and socks, my father's work clothing, a few towels, which we shared and were changed once a week, and washcloths. We put our dirty laundry into a drawstring bag hanging in the broom closet and on the morning my mother did her wash, she would empty the bag onto the basement floor and sort the items into piles: light things, dark stuff, sheets. There was one basket, turquoise plastic mesh, that was used to carry the washed load up to the deck to hang out, or over to the nylon lines strung in the basement to distribute along their lengths. And she was good at laundry. Our clothing emerged from the process spotless. In all the years I've washed my own family's clothing, I've never managed to do as well. Stains, whites that are on the dingy side, dark items shadowed with lint . . . I tell myself and others that it's because I use gentle and biodegradable soaps in order to be kind to the environment, but I wonder.

The dryer was almost never used. It had been bought in an excess of generosity on the part of my father, I think, because I cannot imagine my mother ever asking for a dryer. She was deeply suspicious of them. The way they wore out clothes by tossing them in warm air, the amount of electricity used to run them — my mother often repeated an assertion, confirmed to her by someone who had worked for BC Electric, that of all appliances in the modern home, the dryer was the costliest to operate. It ate up dollars which were hard-won and parted from reluctantly and never frivolously. I think the sheer convenience of the whole process was suspect; and who can blame a woman for thinking this, a woman who had put sheets through a mangle and who had gripped clothes pegs in her teeth while striving to be first on the block to have the wash out on a

Monday morning. I remember once , when I was thirteen, I wanted to hasten the drying of some special pieces of clothing and when my parents had gone for the afternoon, I opened the door of the dryer, intending to use it surreptitiously. She would never know, I reasoned. Imagine my surprise when I discovered a large plastic container of cookies inside the appliance. My brothers and I had wondered where she hid the cookies which she'd bake and then lament that we ate too quickly. We'd searched the kitchen cupboards high and low without any luck. What a clever idea, to hide them in a place where one would never dream to look precisely because it was so little-used or mentioned in the quotidian life of our family. This action spoke of my mother's resourcefulness, her thriftiness, the security of her sense of herself as household queen. Of course I dried my clothes, of course we ate some of the cookies, and of course my mother knew immediately. She knew the minute she entered the house that the dryer had been used. Did it give off ozone or was there a odour of wasted electricity lingering in the air? I'll never know.

One Thanksgiving weekend, my husband and I travelled to Victoria. We had planned to stay with my parents, and help cook a special dinner, an opportunity to see our two younger children who are attending university there. It turned out my parents had already decided to spend the weekend with a brother in another city, but they agreed that we could stay in their house while they were away. I was forty-eight, the age when one often experiences erratic periods. On the ferry to Victoria, I had a sudden unexpected period and realized I would have to wash my jeans as I hadn't packed many clothes for the weekend. Collecting our daughter from her university residence, I casually explained away my sweatpants by saying that I would have to wash my jeans when we returned to my parents' house. She eagerly asked if she could bring along some of her own laundry as she hadn't had a chance to do it that week. I waited while she grabbed a few things to wash.

We took our stuff into the basement, the bare bulbs not quite bright enough in the corner where the appliances stood, and I peered at the worn knob to figure out how to use the washing machine. It was straightforward — no modern control panel here, just a few possible cycles, a couple of temperature choices, and a simple dial for water level. I put in my jeans, a few pairs of my daughter's jeans, some of her underpants, two of her towels, and the small pile of my parents' laundry which I found in the turquoise basket. When the washing machine finished its cycle, I hung the items on the lines in the basement.

A day later most things were dry but the towels were still damp. As we were taking our daughter back to the university, I decided to put them in the dryer to finish them off — her residence room was so small and there was no convenient place for the towels to dry. The dryer wouldn't start. I tried the switch with the door closed, then open. I tried to find the electrical outlet but noticed that there was heavy-duty cable leading into the back of the dryer, which meant it was wired directly to a circuit. I found the electrical panel and saw right away that the circuit was turned off. This was true to my parents' habits of protecting and guarding their possessions, the same habits of mind that imagined hordes of would-be thieves casing their modest house for possible riches. Plexiglass was fitted to many of the windows and could only be removed by a bewildering system of catches and latches. Two-by-fours were bolted to the basement door against entry. And then there were the guns.

I turned the switch on and within fifteen minutes the towels were dry. Removing them from the very small drum, I heard something rattling inside. When the towels were in the basket, I looked into the interior and saw a large rubber ring in the drum. Surely that's the gasket from around the door, I thought. I tried fitting it to where the door met the exterior of the dryer but couldn't manage to get it to stay put. And to be honest, I didn't care to figure it out, thinking that it had must have been off for some time, that it couldn't have come off from my simple act of placing two towels in the drum. And I reasoned with myself that the dryer was probably never used anyway. But while I was rationalizing this to myself, a part of me knew that whatever had happened to the door would be noted immediately and would be blamed on me. My mother's second sight or nose for domestic irregularity would catch out my use (and what would be construed as abuse) of the dryer.

I left a note, along with a pot of chrysanthemums, confessing to using the washing machine. I'd had a spill on the ferry, I said. My parents were due home the day after we left Victoria and it was my hope that everything would repair itself after we left. Of course I knew this was unlikely; but in my mind a zipper closed, or a furrow folded in on itself, keeping its secrets inside — homely as potatoes, or laundry.

The first phone call from my mother came with a question: Had we used the dryer? What had we done to the dryer? I couldn't imagine how they'd known. I'd flipped the switch at the panel, put everything back where it belonged on top — the cleaners, the dank sponges, the ancient tins of pest control remedies, all of which I'd had to push aside to get at the knobs and dials.

I confessed to using the dryer. But nothing had happened, I said. I denied knowledge of any problem.

The gasket, my mother persisted. Why was the gasket inside the drum? I realized that she must have done a thorough search after reading my note. I'd confessed to the washing machine but she knew me, knew there would be more to the story.

I had no idea and said I hadn't noticed, expecting her to see my face redden across the miles. How easy to call shame into being, even in a mother of three, well past girlhood, by the simple use of a telephone. I felt unearned relief at her grudging admission that my father could put the gasket back on the door. Later I told my daughter how I had felt thirteen again, caught breaking the rules of the household. She laughed and told me that on a recent visit to her grandparents, she'd been grilled about the use of the dryer. My mother had even known that we'd dried something blue, and asked what had we dried that was blue? (One of the towels.) And did my daughter know what kind of spill I'd had on the ferry that had required that I wash jeans the first day of a journey? How perversely pleased I was to hear that my secret had been kept.

Two things about that conversation between grandmother and granddaughter made me sad. One was that my mother had actually inspected the lint trap of the dryer to confirm we'd used it and second was my reluctance to tell her the reason for my needing to launder my jeans. Surely she'd have understood something as disruptive as menopause? But she would have travelled prepared, with extra pants (never jeans, of course), and she would not have expected to do laundry in someone else's home, given her notions of host and guest, excess and imposition.

The second phone call came some weeks later. It was my father this time and he made small talk for a moment or two and then: "Can I ask you something without you getting your back up?"

My heart sank. "Yes," I said quietly, wondering why I was being cast as unreasonable (I thought we'd outgrown this particular dance), wondering at what was coming next. I know I am often exasperated at the questions that confound me or embarrass me or perhaps hardest of all, suspect the worst of me, but this time I was determined to remain calm.

"When you used our washing machine, did you have trouble with it?"

I explained again how I had done one load of wash, hung it to dry on the lines for a day and a half, then finished off two towels in the dryer. I told the sequence of events, hoping that it might be seen as something an adult daughter might well expect to do in the family home on a visit.

My father responded with the information that the washing machine hadn't worked properly since their return. He'd tried to remove the agitator to see what was wrong but it wouldn't come off. This washing machine was purchased before I was in my teens and had done the laundry of a family of six for years. I told myself (but not him) that it had surely performed a life's service and might well have decided to give up, but a little voice, the voice of a girl of thirteen, reminded me that it was my use of the appliance that had precipitated its collapse and I must be responsible. A sudden wrinkle of horror collected behind my neck as another voice, the voice of a mother wanting to protect her own reputation, suggested to me, but not to him, that it was probably a pair of my daughter's thong underwear caught under the agitator. When I was told the repairman was coming early the next week, I thought how it would look if and when, by then I was convinced *when*, the tiny underwear, pieces of colourful elastic with a triangle of fabric, came to light, how they would ask themselves over and again how I could allow my daughter to wear such apparel. I would fail in their eyes as a mother, even though my delightful girl gave them such pleasure on her visits, was far nicer to them than I managed to be, brushing over criticisms and disapproval with ease and grace.

When I was the age that my daughter is now, and my mother the age that I am at present, there was an incident in our household that I have never forgotten. When we moved from a farmhouse in the Fraser Valley to the house my parents live in now, when I was fourteen, I asked, not unreasonably, what one should do with used sanitary napkins. In the farmhouse, with its ancient septic system (and as with most septic systems), it was considered a crime to put anything but toilet paper down the toilet. But in the newer house, I was told that one could simply flush the napkin down. So I did. After several years of this, the drains backed up. Even though there was a map in the basement showing the supposed location of the septic tank, the tank wouldn't be found. Finally, on a weekend, it was decided to call someone to fix the problem after tins of drain opener had failed to work. A man came. He wore hip-waders and a rubber jacket. He dug and skewered with a long steel rod, skewered and dug, until he found the tank some distance from its mapped location. He spent some time dragging debris out of the pipes leading into the tank and he divulged to my parents that the main culprits in the blocked drains were, of course, the sanitary napkins, and a long elastic bandage left from my brother's ankle injury, though how that had ended up in the toilet was anyone's guess, and how the napkins had ended up there was entirely my fault. The cost of this Sunday emergency visit — time and a half — was repeated to anyone who would listen and some, like me, who didn't want to hear it yet again. Taken aside, I was reprimanded for my carelessness and when I said what I had been told to do, no one could remember giving me permission to dispose of the evidence of my periods in such a way. My cheeks heat up now, remembering.

In thinking about this, I wonder at the elevation of appliances in my family home to the role of something resembling household gods, the laundry shrine in the basement, of course, lit by a dim bulb, and the large television in its wooden cabinet taking up an entire corner of the living room, crowned with a combination lamp and candy dish resembling ducks in flight. My parents gave my husband and me a washing machine as a wedding present. It was my "machine". In the weekly telephone call, in those years, I would be asked how my "machine" was working. It took me a time or two to deduce just what machine they meant for I'd lived away from that household for many years. I had, after all, an electric typewriter with which I wrote books, I had a sewing machine for piecing together quilts, I shared a lawnmower and a car with my husband. We had a printing press. But what a difference an automatic washing machine must have made to my mother's household activities when one was finally purchased for her and I think it must have been a pleasure for them to save me from that early drudgery. No need to stand by the old wringer washer to ease clothing through the mangle, no fearful watching of young children playing in its vicinity — someone always knew someone who knew a child whose arm had been flattened by being drawn through while a mother watched horrified. And yet I took our appliances so much for granted. And who wouldn't? Once, when our washing machine refused to drain (a baby's sock stuck in a hose — It was this memory of how a small item could cause such chaos that made me think of my daughter's thong), I had to take each item out and wring it into the bathtub by hand. Socks and diapers were simple but jeans and sheets took forever. It could take a big chunk out of a woman's day, or life, to have to do such things on a regular basis. On a fine day when the wind blew and the sun shone, it was a pleasure to stand on the wooden stoop to peg out sheets and shirts, to see the pillowcases billow and fly. But it was never the measure of my worthiness, as mother, as homemaker, to manage to dry our laundry in this way, rain or shine.

Our first washing machine and dryer did not last forever. After something like fifteen or eighteen years, and the collective daily laundry of a family of five (for I washed clothes when the baskets were full, not waiting for a particular day), they broke down. For me, it was not a tragedy, not a sign of failure, to see the old ones dragged out to the truck for removal to the dump and new ones arrive. My son reminds me that when the new dryer was delivered, my parents stood by it after my husband had eased it into its place under the stairs — we have no basement, no room set aside for the sole purpose of doing laundry; our washer and dryer are installed in a cubbyhole under the stairs, with folding doors to close them off from the household — and made sure it was properly plugged into its special outlet and they touched it almost reverently, saying to each other, "A beautiful machine." Its capacity must have seemed huge to them, I am thinking, remembering the tiny drum of their dryer, surrounded by a huge heating element responsible for using such volumes of electricity, the cogs and wheels of the meter whirring and spinning so quickly that they must have clutched their wallets fearfully. How times change, how we change in our expectations of what we are willing to do, and what we refuse.

So now I am waiting for the third phone call, the one which will draw the inevitable link between my mothering skills and the damage done to their appliances. Again I will feel myself to have disappointed my parents for being so cavalier with the plumbing of others, for my profligacy with the electrical dollar. From this distance, I can see the repairman hold up the thong, maybe the magenta one edged in soft pink, and the shock on my parents' faces. In their lives they will probably never be burgled, never have their home invaded by young men wearing balaclavas and carrying steel pipes, bursting through the plexiglass to carry out…well, what? There are no small electronics in that house, apart from a tape player we sent to them after learning that my mother had to sit in their truck in order to listen to gift tapes of a favourite singer, the idea of actually purchasing a boom box unthinkable to them. No computers, no microwave, no discman, no dvd player. Yet habit has them fitting the two-by-fours into slots against the basement door, has them affixing the plexiglass over their patio doors before sleep. They take solace in the knowledge of my father's gun collection tucked away in a secret place, locked, ammunition stored elsewhere, although I suspect a weapon might be kept closer to hand in defiance of Canada's gun law, just in case. And habit has the dryer sitting aging and powerless in the corner of the basement until a switch is activated and it can groan and wheeze, holding in its trap a cloud of blue lint as evidence, has the washing machine idle six days out of seven, just waiting for the prodigal daughter to use it in secret before it seizes up and refuses to work. Girls become women, move away, become mothers themselves, yet the faintest whiff of laundry soap, a crackle of forbidden electricity, and the years disappear like difficult stains.

∾

Scouring Rush

WE ARE STANDING on the edge of Haskins Creek, watching the coho as they make their way up the narrow water course to the spawning beds further along. The water is very cold — it's December, after all — and clear, though that is deceptive. I know that this creek is teeming with aquatic insects. One year, in February, my daughter and her science partner Gloria spent many hours sampling the creek water, itemizing its contents for a science fair project on water quality.

They were fifteen years old. They liked boy bands, fashion magazines, horror movies and junk food. But on Saturday mornings they'd put on their oldest clothes and high rubber boots, take up their nets and sieves, buckets, jars, books and charts, and I'd drive them down to the creek to conduct their field work. They were very diligent. Each sampling took a couple of hours. To keep warm, I'd walk the area, observing the plants and watching for birds. An American dipper, or ouzel (the name I preferred), would frequently bob above the water, or else stand on a rock or partially submerged log before doing deep knee bends as it dipped into the water for stray fish eggs or the same aquatic insects and larvae the girls were seeking. Sometimes I'd see it run along the creek bottom, a depth of twelve inches at least, a sight that always delighted me. They are truly wonderful to see — pert little grey birds, smaller than robins, who go about these exercises without taking notice of anyone watching. And there were often common mergansers, males sleek, the females with their chestnut crests, at the creek mouth, winter wrens in the underbrush, ravens loud in the winter sky.

I loved looking at the stands of various equisetum, or horsetails, growing in among the salmonberry. They appear all along the creekside, the fertile stalks coming up in early spring, brown, scaly and lacking chlorophyll; then the vegetative stems emerging a little later, green and branched. In fall, winter and late spring, you could still see the shapes of the summer's plants pressed into mud here and there. When I was a child, I was told these plants were around at the time of dinosaurs and I always wondered how that was known. Fossil records show a huge number of horsetails, all looking much the same as their modern counterparts. Some of the prehistoric equisetums were as large as trees but one particular fossil of *Annularia* (roughly 300 million years old) shows the delicate branching whorls of the vegetative stems, exactly as the plant grows in the twenty-first century, and another, of *Equisetum florissantense* (35 million years old, from an area in Colorado buried by volcanic eruptions), shows the segmented stalk of a scouring rush, every detail as precise as though the plant was growing on Haskins Creek and not imprinted in rock. There is something simple and primitive about these plants, especially the fertile stalks, pale and scaled, their long rhizomes netted through the soil.

The horsetail cousins, *Equisetum hyemale*, or scouring rushes, grow in the same kind of area but aren't as common. They are not branched but appear jointed, like bamboo without leaves; their sheaths are often grey to black, with dark teeth. If you run your finger along a length of scouring rush, it will feel rough to the touch. This is because the outer cell walls are impregnated with silicon and this is what gives this particular equisetum its common name.

Haskins Creek empties into Sakinaw Lake which eventually empties into the ocean via a short run of creek. I love the estuary. It isn't grand like the estuary of a great and turbulent river but it has the charm of something hidden and contained. There's often a population of mew gulls in the small bay. We've seen eagles on the bluffs where the remains of an old donkey engine and its spar attest to the use of Sakinaw Lake as a holding pond for a logging concern in the years when the lake opened at low tide to the sea.

How lovely a word: estuary. The *s* sound at the front of your mouth, then the wide opening. The rush of vowels. The tidal swoosh. Saying it, I can see those gulls feeding in the rich confluence of fresh and salt water. In the estuary at the end of Sakinaw Lake, we've collected oysters from the undersides of rocks; seen salmon flipping themselves out of the bay, a seal watching them from further out; found bear scat on the shore, thick with berries; seen the fierce western terrestrial garter snakes fishing at the edge of the water, taking bullheads or even small crabs, then swimming away with them in their mouths. Once, I found a portion of a slate fish knife which had tumbled down from the exposed midden layer and knew that other people, perhaps centuries earlier, had taken the same pleasure in the sunlight, the bleached logs, the smell of mud as the tide receded.

In a good year for returns, the coho fill narrow Haskins Creek in December. The year the girls sampled the waters in February, they caught an infant salmon, or alevin, still connected to its eggsac. Of course they released it immediately back into the cold waters and gravel bottom of its nativity, but I wondered if it would survive any number of perils — dippers, leeches, larger fish in the lake it would have to swim across before entering the ocean at the estuary — and live out its adult life in the Pacific waters before navigating its way home. The adults in December in their deep burgundy and green colours are such a small percentage of those who set off three or four years earlier. Still it is a moving sight, those fish idling in the creek's shallows, digging the redds with their strong tails, and eventually drifting listless and spent while eagles and bears wait to feed on their nutritious corpses. And the big cedars also ready to feed, though of course differently, and over a longer period of time, as the animals distribute the important nutrients to the soil.

The process of navigation is still one of nature's great mysteries although some pieces of the puzzle are known. It has always been assumed that salmon navigate in part by smell, that the waters of their natal creeks are known to them by smell, and that there is an olfactory imprint on the smolts as they leave that home stream. I imagine the great tangle of odours in the vast ocean as all the tiny creeks and larger rivers empty their waters in all seasons. And then I figure in the pollutants introduced into those waterways. It has also been thought that fish navigate, like birds, by means of celestial readings, a perception of the sun's azimuth as well as the constellations. But what is now known is that fish, like migrating birds, have magnetite cells in their heads, containing crystals of iron oxide, which align with magnetic north. It's believed that these interior compasses are "set" at the fish's entry into the ocean, along with that olfactory imprint. I imagine them drawn irresistibly home, as we have been drawn to beloved places, to land or water, and in this case, the nearby creek.

Those cold February days the girls filled buckets with water and then used small dip nets and screened frames to see what kinds of aquatic insects might be found in a stream. They were sampling three creeks and hypothesized that this one, Haskins Creek, would be the cleanest, with the highest oxygen levels, supporting the most variety of insect life. They found mayfly larvae, dragonfly nymphs, leeches, stonefly nymphs, waterboatmen, a few stray crayfish, and a variety of caddisfly larvae — depending on the species of caddis fly, the larvae conceal themselves in cases they built out of bits of shell, stick, grains of sand or plant stalks. It was fascinating to find the clusters of detritus and then to discover a tiny bristled head emerging from the entrance. The girls made lists of what they found which they entered later onto databases.

When I was a girl, I loved ponds and creeks. I remember a quick cold run of water that tumbled down a hill near our home in Spryfield, near Halifax. I would have been eight or nine that year. I followed that creek as far as I could up to the woods where it must have continued on to Kidstone Lake. There was a pond where we skated in winter and where frogs could be caught in summer; trails linked these areas, some of them wilder than others. I was idling along one of the less-travelled trails one day with the family Labrador, Star, when a man suddenly appeared in front of us. He had a strange look on his face, not scary exactly but a bit crazed. And his trousers were open in the front to show his penis hanging out. He stood dead-centre on the trail in a way that I know now was meant to be threatening. But Star simply walked around him, not interested in what he was exposing, and I took her cue, passing him as far to one side of the trail as I could. I didn't want to be impolite so I made eye contact and said hello as I passed him. I don't recall if he said anything to me but he didn't follow us. I remember making a mental note to myself to stay off the more remote trails unless I was with someone else.

Years later, I wonder how I could have been so calm. But those were different times. We were put out in the morning to play and told not to come back to the house until lunch-time, or dinner, even, if we had a packed lunch to take with us. The warnings were vague. Be careful of cars, don't play on the highway, don't take rides from strangers. But politeness to adults was also stressed. So a stranger encountered on a path, exposing himself, and possibly dangerous, must be treated with courtesy. I remember no direct warnings involving possible sexual interference though once, passing Beacon Hill Park with my mother when we lived in the Fairfield neighbourhood in Victoria, I saw a child's panties in the bushes along the sidewalk. My mother got very upset and said how she hated to see things like that. From the distance of years and my own current state of motherhood and knowledge of abuse in the world at large, I know (I *think* I know) what she meant — although she certainly didn't elaborate then and left me mystified. I tried then to work out how a child's underwear might end up in the bushes and could only conclude that an accident had occurred, the child had wet herself, and had been too frightened to return home with pee-stained panties. My mother's response somehow fed into this conclusion and for years I thought the worst that might happen to a child was loss of bladder control.

Sometimes I've thought of following Haskins Creek to its source. I know where it comes down the mountain and passes through a culvert to travel under the highway and down the long slope to where it enters Sakinaw Lake. It travels rough terrain, rocky mountainside, deep woods, broken up here and there by logging roads, most of them put to bed. More stalwart people than I hike this area regularly. In the newspapers there are invitations to join a group exploring this watershed or that, with lists of what to bring: compasses, maps, waterproof gear, a hearty lunch. I know from participating in one or two of these events that great ground is covered, that people are generally good-natured though earnest in the extreme, and that often there is a tendency among those involved to one-up the others in various fields of expertise. One cannot simply *be* in nature but must make an effort to hike further, know more species, list birds, flowers, trees in a knowledgeable way. In contrast, on the expeditions with the girls, I saw them immersed in the joy of discovery as they lifted their containers of water to the shore and eagerly looked to see what might be seen. Then, remembering what they were supposed to be doing, they began counting, itemizing, separating. Following the creek to its source strikes me as within the realm of categorizing. Maybe I am happier not entirely knowing the where and the why but loving rather the mystery of arrival. That creek in Spryfield came down through open woods, eastern woods, not like our dense coastal forests with waist-high salal to impede one's progress. And there were trails, I recall, and I have written of their own unexpected perils.

Scouring rush lends an elegance to its setting by the creek. Tall and beautifully articulated, it stands in the soft mud like a moment in a Japanese woodcut– there is a lovely print of a bamboo forest that could almost be the rushes by this creek presented from the perspective of the ground, looking up at the elegant stalks. In all seasons the scouring rush is poised by water. A kingfisher scolding in the alders nearby enlivens this scene, as do the crane flies alighting on a leaf, a log.

And the scene is forever animated for me by memory of those girls and their buckets, their hip-waders. My thumb rough on the edge of scouring rush, my eyes alert for dippers and the occasional heron in the shallow water at the lake's edge. The creek bank is a place where I've found the earliest blooming salmonberry, the tiny buds showing cerise, unfolding like silk. When I was a child, I loved the story of Princess Furball, who carried her gowns in a walnut shell, opening it to reveal dresses woven to resemble the sun, the moon and the stars. Beauty is often contained in unlikely vessels — the tiny black commas in jelly that become tree frogs, green as emeralds; or specks of black seed growing to poppies, each unfurling from its pod like the gowns of the princess but the colour of sunsets. The process of transformation or metamorphosis — do we consciously take our cue from nature: the turning of the seasons, the development of bud to flower, egg to frog, the smolts in Haskins Creek heading to sea and then returning, guided by stars, the smell of water, the presence of iron oxide in their brains? One theory of aboriginal songlines suggests that people painted their bodies with iron oxide pigment which acted as a navigational aid, working magnetically with the singing to guide individuals home. I think we are more deeply connected to nature than we would sometimes like to believe. We begin our lives within an amniotic sac within a chorionic sac — the fluids and mucus of these environments not unlike those which contain amphibians. The yolk-sac we adhere to in our first four weeks, (the sac of the young alevin emerging from the gravel of their natal streams), our one-chambered heart at the beginnings of our lives before our backbone develops, our eyes without their lens: we could be salmon waiting in the rushes, sand dollars with small spines paused in the clean sand of the intertidal zone.

Scouring rush, like its relatives the horsetails, has been used for centuries, maybe millennia, as an abrasive. The sixteenth-century English herbalist Gerard reports its usefulness for scouring pewter and wood. Comb-makers and fletchers used it for both rubbing and polishing. Coastal native people used it like sandpaper for arrow shafts, feast dishes and Interior peoples combined it with salmon slime to polish stone pipes and arrowheads and even their fingernails. Nicolas Culpepper, a later English herbalist, and the ancient Greek physician Galen both thought highly of it as a means to staunch bleeding, and the ashes of the plant were used to cure kidney and bladder ailments.

I think of an estuary as a place where metamorphoses becomes meaningful. Twice a day, the ocean is refreshed by sweet water, the mudflats are exposed to the sun then covered again. Salt marshes have a lengthier opportunity to remain intact but then a seasonal high tide will wash up and over. Any plant temporarily growing there, seeded capriciously by wind or carried in bird droppings, which cannot withstand the salinity of a tide, will not survive. The beds of eelgrass provide shelter for many small marine organisms which move through their life-cycles as predictably as tides — crustaceans, jellyfish, diatoms and algae — and geese feed in the grass with their young. When we enter the water ourselves, it is as though we become other than what we are, linked to the marine world through the saline properties of our blood. Cold at first, our bodies adapt to the sea, our pulse echoing the surge and retreat of tides. For a time, in utero, a human embryo resembles the fertilized egg of a sea-urchin. Little row of gill-arches, primitive heart, no face — for a moment, it could be a fish, a salamander curling its tail behind it. Perhaps this is what our cells remember as we float in salt water, drifting through beds of kelp like eels. And it doesn't surprise me to remember, when carrying my own three children inside me, how water was the element I longed for, either immersing myself in the sea or a warm bath, feeling a buoyancy lost to me on land. As my babies moved in their journey towards the air and light, I was yearning backwards, inwards, to my own residency in the body of my mother. And before that, some primordial deep.

The passage from aquatic larvae to mature caddisfly or mayfly; from egg to adult salmon; from cluster of glistening spawn clinging to reeds into the beautiful red-legged frogs of these coastal forests — it happens in such a brief period. Our own human transition seems so much longer and more difficult. There are days now when I feel every second of my half century on earth and see the process of age at work on my face and my body. Was I ever that young, I asked myself, when presented with the glow of those young women at work in the creek. But what I have come to know is that at each subsequent stage of personal development, the new form contains the nucleus of the previous within it. My girlhood self, with that dreamy personality and hopes and attachments to animals, is still resident in this older body. It's as though I carry her in the way I carried my babies, tenderly and carefully, though she is not waiting to be born but anticipating our mutual death one day when the memory of who she was will accompany me, stiff-jointed and grey-haired, to our common end.

Those girls, counting their leeches and nymphs, the larvae of stoneflies, left school to enter university, one in biology and one studying the ancient texts of the Romans and Greeks. In time, they might enter the rich stream of motherhood, embryos developing inside them, the intricate spiral of the DNA code tracing the passage of families throughout history and landscape. Who they were in those days of sampling water in Haskins Creek, surrounded by salmonberry, scouring rush, young alders in the muck of the creek's overflow, will travel in mysterious ways to future generations. Someone, finding their boot prints in the mud of the creek, might wonder at the swift passage of time or the long moment of eternity as the salmon find their way to the gravel beds of their birth.

～

Slow Food

You are writing this after spending two and a half hours in Powell River in between your ferry from Earls Cove and this ferry to Little River on Vancouver Island. You could write an essay about Powell River; you had this thought the minute you boarded the ferry. It would be about a place you never thought you'd write about. You could call it "Slow Food". You pull out your journal and your fountain pen. It helps you forget that this is an old ferry in an aging fleet, one of which rammed into an island and sank just three days earlier.

DRIVING FROM SALTERY Bay where the Earls Cove ferry with its load of seven cars docked, in mist quickly becoming rain, I am struck as I have been on every visit by what has happened to Powell River over the years. Visiting there in the seventies, I'd thought it seemed prosperous. I remember lots of talk about the mill, jobs, the economy. But this time there are at least three small dead motels along the highway, one covered in what looked like aluminum foil. Another one is being consumed by blackberry canes. It has to do with the time of year, trees in bud but not leafy yet, so that every building stands out with its worn timbers showing, not softened by green. Each abandoned motel is grey with rain, as though holiday-makers and travelling salesmen just stopped coming and the buildings turned their sad faces from the road. An exception is the Marland but it's hardly contemporary. Tiny blue and white cubes, no pool, no hot tub, no decks hanging over the sea. John and I talk about how a movie could be made, set in the late fifties or early sixties, a murder mystery, with an investigating detective coming from afar to stay at the Marland Motel with its *"Clean modern units, some with kitchenettes"*, each unit, maybe ten feet by ten feet, arranged around a traffic circle. The gal reporter he would become involved with might live with her mother in a faded pink house on Joyce Avenue. The reporter would visit at the Marland after dark, parking her Valiant just up the road, and the two would drink rye-and-7 from plastic cups provided in the tiny bathroom, each sanitarily wrapped for their protection. I imagine chenille bedspreads and the smell of better days.

Anyway, I like Powell River for its quirky pride — the ocean-life mosaics set into the sidewalks along Marine Drive but now chipped and repaired with cement, the hopeful neon, the friendly young woman in the toll booth at the ferry terminal where we park and then walk up to explore the lower town. A bus passes, *Welcome, Bienvenue, #2 to Grief Point.* (I try to make this into a haiku and it almost works.) Although it had been raining on the drive in, the skies clear just enough so that we can amble along and not worry about getting soaked. I was cold when I left our house for the first ferry, cold on the ferry itself, but now I put my gloves away, open my jacket.

There is the electrical shop with the dirty but useable generators and alternators in the window, a window I had noticed the last time we were in Powell River, back in December, because someone had hung a few Christmas lights around its frame. Peering in this time, I see the girlie calendar hanging on the back wall and a few men standing around, their hands in their pockets. No one is in a hurry.

We walk past the employment centre (surely this was a gift or craft shop once, years ago, when we did this same trip?), past the Love Shop with the little wispy bits of lingerie hanging in the window and a sign promising a good selection of adult toys. Past the pawn shops, the loan centres. We stop at a bakery, order a cup of dark roast coffee for my husband and two shots of espresso for myself. Long or short? I am asked, and I reply, Just the two shots please. John's mug is brought right away and the young woman works the steaming machines for a few minutes before bringing me two small blue cups, each holding a generous measure of espresso. I smile, drink one, then the other.

Up the hill to the menswear shop where a beautiful silk shirt in the window catches my husband's eye and where he enters the shop, tries on the shirt, and buys it in a moment of uncharacteristic extravagance while the salesman holds forth about the pleasures of small-town life (we had mentioned Merritt and that set him off). Next door I admire, but don't try on, a jewelled bustier and goth-influenced cloak, though I wish I had special occasions for both.

At the bookstore we are pleased to see a display of our own books with a sign saying Local Authors, even though we live a ferry ride away and we've never been asked to the town's Writers Festival held every April. And when I pay for the books I have chosen, there is no delighted moment of recognition as my name is noticed on the credit card slip but for this I am actually grateful.

Down to Marine again where we are surprised to see a new bookstore in a storefront, gracious wood-framed window newly restored, so we open the door and enter. Wooden bookshelves, tidy and uncluttered, line the perimeter walls and a number of tables, neatly set with cutlery and wine glasses, are in the centre of the room. I quickly realize that this is heaven. Or The Kitchen Table, more precisely, a place specializing in books about food, some of them cookbooks, some treatises on gastronomy, all in excellent condition, first editions and rare editions alike. I choose two MFK Fishers I haven't read and one Diana Kennedy and restrain myself from also buying Artemis Cooper's biography of Elizabeth David and other wonderful volumes I devoured as a young woman learning about the joys of cheese, soups, ripe figs and mellow wine with peaches. There are also dated and numbered bottles of olive oil. I wonder, I say, if I will find a little tin of La Chinata paprika as mine is almost empty. And turn: there it is, the last one. A man in shorts and new wave glasses emerges from a little kitchen at the back to say, "You're in time for lunch!" which is a choice of Louisiana gumbo and another soup (we can smell garlic, fresh parsley, rich stock . . .). He tells us he has recently relocated to Powell River from sunny California to cook and sell books. "Some days I do menudo and posole," he confides as he washes his hands before adding up my purchases. We decline lunch — we have a ferry to catch and anyway I ate a large cookie with my two cups of espresso — but then passing the Italian delicatessen, two doors down from The Kitchen Table on our way back to the car, we enter and ask for sandwiches to go.

"Choose anything you like from the display case", we are told. So prosciutto salami and gorgonzola; and the man cuts fresh Calabrian Bakery buns from Vancouver and sets to work. He brings an open mason jar to us to ask if we'd like his parents' marinated green tomatoes in olive oil with herbs instead of mustard. It smells like summer in March. He takes twenty-five minutes to fill the buns with the meat, the cheese, the luscious relish, during which time I put a tube of tomato doppio on the counter, 2 tins of olives stuffed with anchovies, limonata, some perciati pasta with cooking instructions only in Italian but I'm able to translate — Cottura: 9 minuti normale, 7 minuti al dente. I can almost taste them, maybe with a thick ragu, shaved parmesan, lots of garlic. And at the last minute, I buy seeds for Ruccola Coltivata and Basilico Napoletano a Foglia di Lattugo, and again I feel sure I can figure out the semina, the distanza . . . I can almost taste some of the basil in the sauce for the pasta, a salad of the arugula alongside, though I know it will be months before I can cut the greens from my garden.

And finally we walk back to the ferry parking lot where our car is first in line. We say again to each other that we don't know what it is about Powell River but we think we could live here, the air soft, the food slow and long simmering and available with excellent things to read, untold erotic possibilities from a shop with beaded curtains, and even as we are saying this, the cactus sign is being carried to the sidewalk in front of La Casita Mexican Restaurant where the chili pepper lights strung around it speak of southern heat, of *churros* dusted with cinnamon sugar, of cold beer on a hot day in June. Already we are planning our return.

∾

PAPERWEIGHT

ONE DAY, WHEN I was washing dishes in the kitchen, I overheard my mother telling my children a small story, a fragment of a story, about a paperweight on her mother's desk. It was filled with flowers. Whenever my mother dusted that room, she would linger at the desk, looking at the ornament which she knew was precious to her mother. I heard her say that the paperweight was linked in her mind with a story she'd read about some children on a mission to Norway where they had to deliver a paperweight, though she couldn't remember to whom or to what. And I thought, listening to her, that I had never really had a clear picture of her in childhood, that this story made me see a girl in a room with a duster, carefully cleaning a globe of glass, her imagination at play.

My mother's childhood in Halifax always seemed bleak in the telling. Born to an unmarried mother, given up at birth, taken into foster care by a widow who never adopted her and wouldn't allow other families to adopt her; but provided a home in a boarding house, an older foster sister, an abusive foster brother. A girl who was so obviously grateful for so little. We first visited that house when my father was transferred to Halifax from Victoria for two years and my mother was still trying to please — giving us stern warnings about behaviour, buying the chocolate ginger that her foster-mother loved, smoothing the edges of my father's temper so that the household would think she had made a good marriage. And she had, for the most part. But it was a household with tight rules and observations: about children, about men, about the world around it. (I remember warnings from Grammy — we were instructed to call her Grammy — about swimming in the public pool on the nearby Common because of the black children . . .) We stayed in the boarding house while looking for a house of our own to rent and my brothers and I slept in cots in an attic room. The wood in that house was very dark and polished. There were miles of lace made by Grammy, who was blind, and who read our faces with her fingertips, her lap filled with reels of crochet cotton.

There was a birth certificate, apparently, with the names of both parents, though my mother never contacted them. And a paper trail leading to them, to their homes, their new lives. My mother didn't want to intrude. But imagine giving up a child and never tracing the life of that child. Imagine never knowing if she grew up happy, had a family of her own, children who would have been true grandchildren, linked by blood and genetic material. I think of the helix spiralling towards them and never quite reaching them, lost in the space between city streets. Telephones mute, mail boxes empty.

There was a foster sister and brother, as I've said. The brother was bad-tempered, possibly abusive, and went on to have daughters of his own. We never met the brother or his children. The girls were spoken of by Grammy and Aunt H.

in a way I'm certain my brothers and I were never spoken of
— Kimmy and Bobbie, two girls, whom I imagined had hair
like Shirley Temple, to go with those names. Saddle shoes and
matching cardigans. Aunt H. kept in touch with us after we left
Halifax, even visited us on the west coast once we'd returned
to Victoria. I remember her observing, frankly, of my father,
"A.'s got a bad temper, doesn't he?" In that house of women in
Halifax, one who had never married, the other widowed in 1917
and dying in 1968, a man's anger was something unknown.
The temper was a product of running a difficult slide viewer so
that we could see Aunt H.'s photographs: her Volvo; herself in
headscarf, on a terrace in Yugoslavia; her travelling companion
(a woman called Peg) tricked out in pedal pushers, posing by a
stone church in eastern Europe; some lobster traps; a headland
in Maine. I remember how my mother set the table for her
foster-sister's breakfast — our old plates (resinware of some
sort) and mugs on the daily mats, and a special mat set with
china plate and cup and saucer. Such an obvious attempt for
praise. It embarrassed me then and my cheeks warm now,
remembering.

There was a time when I thought of Aunt H. as a true aunt,
although remote. She showed some interest in me when I was
a growing girl. It was knowing later that she'd kept my mother
in her place that caused me to remove the overlay of intimacy
and made me reconsider the use of "aunt" when I thought of
her at all. She had shown my father her father's diaries — he'd
been a physician on the Grenfell Mission Ships — and a few
other papers which my father was very interested in. So was my
son, later on when he was taking a degree in Canadian history
and dreamed of doing something with them. But they were

hoarded, along with affection. No provisions were made for them so that when she died, in an advanced state of dementia, no one mentioned the papers or knew what had happened to them.

The paperweight was filled with flowers. Was it a piece of millefiore, I wondered? I've read about the process for creating those paperweights filled with a thousand flowers, developed in Venice in the late fifteenth century. Rods of glass of varying colours were put together to form a design and then fused into a single rod which was then stretched, cut into sections, and sliced into beads, each the same. These would be arranged in a pleasing pattern and enclosed in a dome of clear glass. It sounds like something that would have come from that house — Grammy's husband had been the son of a sugar trader who moved between Jamaica and Scotland. The family home was on the island of Mull but the children lived in Jamaica as well. Boats moving back and forth across the Atlantic often result in gifts.

And what would the paperweight have held down? Bills, almost certainly, and perhaps letters from the far-flung brother, from the linen salesman from Belfast who came to Halifax regularly to sell linens to hotels and who boarded with my "grandmother". She kept boarders after the death of her husband, who'd worked hard treating the wounded during the Halifax explosion of 1917 and had been worn out afterwards, succumbing to the Spanish flu.

I am surprised at my bitterness now. As a child, I thought that grandparents were a commodity as remote as ice-bergs. My father's parents were very old. Their English was heavily accented — my grandfather was from Bukovina and my grandmother from Bohemia — and we barely knew them, visiting once a year to stand in front of them so they could see our height, our resemblances or not to scores of cousins. There were no affable elders like the ones in books who wrote letters and sent silly gifts like puzzles or taffy. Ours sent a little money, and practical things like pyjamas were purchased by our mother; dutiful thank-you notes were sent to Edmonton. Spending a few weeks in that dark quiet house in Halifax seemed like an opportunity to bask in the warmth of a grandmother, an aunt; warmth that was not forthcoming, not then nor ever after. And if it was not given us, then imagine what it must have been like to be the foundling taken in with a birth certificate but no other visible connection to a family? They *must* have felt something for her. Any small baby I've held has filled my heart with tenderness that could easily become love. And having seen my own children respond to praise and rich love, seen the good generous people they've become in a house of affection, I can only grieve and feel a kind of loss for my mother's childhood. A story is told of her "brother" buying ice-cream for a group of other foster children in the household, but not for her. Another story tells of Aunt H. informing her bluntly about menstruation. You could say it was the times but when has love been restricted to particular decades, to particular households?

In the last years of Aunt H.'s life, a neighbour helped her to cope with her loss of memory, took her grocery shopping and helped transport her to medical appointments. My mother went a few times to visit from her home on the opposite coast, to the same house she had grown up in, and called the neighbour regularly for news. She was troubled by her foster-sister's descent into dementia but always absolved herself by saying,

"But what can I do? There's not a thing I can do." I made some suggestions — a call to the Public Health services in Halifax (in fact, Aunt H. was a retired Public Health nurse) to alert them to the fact that she was not eating or heating her house properly although she lived on a good pension and had money put away. There was a man friend for some of her later life but no mention of him once she'd entered the blurred world of dementia. I always wondered why she never married and my mother has mentioned in recent years that she'd had suitors, but whenever they got serious about a relationship, her mother would scare them off, afraid of being left alone in her later years. So her daughter pursued a career, did a graduate degree, and lived in the family house until she suffered a heart attack in the last year of her life and was moved to a care facility.

When she died, there was a tiny sum of money left to my mother, with everything else going to the neighbour. The neighbour, not an unkind woman from all accounts, asked my mother if there was anything she would like to have as a keepsake and my mother remembered two things — a charm bracelet with tokens of Aunt H.'s travels and the paperweight. The neighbour, living now in Aunt H.'s house, having previously lived in a basement suite next door, said she would send the bracelet but that her husband "had taken a shine to the paperweight." A small thing, perhaps valuable, but containing within it flowers, the memory of Norway, a story I've been unable to trace.

So yes, I'm surprised at my bitterness, my sense of sadness for my mother, anger at the neighbour's husband who inherited everything but a charm bracelet and a thousand dollars but who wouldn't pass along a paperweight with its cargo of flowers and memories.

My husband went on a trip while I was musing about this and returned with a gift for me, a hand-blown paperweight with a beautiful sea anemone inside. There are five tentacles of pink and blue glass. I believe that it was made with rods of glass, like in millefiore but the rods have been hollowed or opened rather than stretched. I know that sea anemones are carnivorous — we see them on the local beaches, at the intertidal zone, waving their tentacles in the air for prey. Touching them with a finger, we feel the faint suction, then see them retract. I know they are territorial and can clone themselves so that often a colony will develop which consists of genetically identical anemones; when another colony encroaches, those on the periphery engage in battles to defend their little area of rock. Maybe they are defending their genetic integrity. Looking at my paperweight, I imagine that something has been captured inside it, something precious and rare.

If Grammy had allowed my mother to be adopted, as was the possibility, then I wonder if things would have been different. A girl growing up *wanted*, cherished, given a name with stories attached, a semblance of history, a role defined and formal. There would have been family documents to hold down firmly with a paperweight, a place for her in the long inheritance of objects and anecdotes, someone to say, *We chose you out of all possible babies to be our own dear girl.* And yet Grammy must have felt something for the infant she took into her home, a child who dusted a paperweight, who had enough imagination to make a connection between a story and an object, and who surely deserved the fullness of maternal love and joy.

There is a point in the development of a human embryo when it closely resembles the fertilized egg of a sea urchin. The adult sea urchins discharge their eggs and sperm into the sea and fertilization is more random than in other species. The resulting larvae might be the product of egg and sperm from individuals existing miles away from each other. I keep the exoskeleton of a sea urchin on my shelf, run my fingers over its bristles. There is one type of sea anemone called the brooding anemone, named for the habit of the fertilized eggs developing into embryos which attach themselves to the pedal disc of the animal — the base from which the lovely tentacles reach — where they grow, migrating away as they mature. In the life histories of both these intertidal animals is something of my mother's story, my story — the nature of infants and their development, with or without parental nurture. The more I think about it, the more I realize how little I know about the weight of love.

As a child in Nova Scotia, I loved to look into tide pools on family excursions to the shore and still do this on the western beaches near where I live, where sea anemones take in their food, the light suction of their tentacles trying my finger, then retreating. On my desk, a paperweight containing a perfect sea anemone, created from molten glass, pink and blue, its tentacles open and ready. I take it in my palm and gaze into its depths, looking for something. It is the world made perfect, suspended in clear glass. If I look into it long enough, will it tell me the secrets of memory, offer the moment when a daughter might be reunited with a mother, show me how the heart might beat like a tide washing in, gathering its embryos home?

∾

Phantom Limb

Can thou lift up thy voice to the clouds, that abundance of
waters may cover thee? . . .

WE HAD OUR old dog put to sleep on March 24, 1998. As near
as we could tell, she was thirteen, maybe a month or two more
or shy. We got her when she was about a year old and for the
past twelve years she was my companion. We walked together
daily; she'd wait for the walks with great patience, finding a
place to lie near the house to keep my comings and goings in
view. When I look out the window now, I find myself seeing
her momentarily, a trick of the light, the heart. I've heard her
barking in the night and then realized it couldn't be her; I lie in
the darkness, feeling the loss of her as physically as one might
miss a hand, an eye.

We got her by responding to an ad in the local newspaper:
Lab Shepherd cross, one year old, free to good home. When I
called, I was told to come to the Sechelt Indian Reserve, and
then find the house across from the soccer field. I drove down
the coast with my son in our old brown truck, the ad clipped

and hidden in my wallet like a charm. My husband John had said, Don't bring back a dog unless it's perfect. He didn't mean purebred or professionally trained; he meant don't bring it home if it bites, if it has serious health problems, vices. We'd had a lovely old dog who kept the deer from our garden, who was gentle with our three small children, who was loyal and easygoing. When she died, we were still building our house, our children were all toddlers, we were both writing books, and John taught on two campuses, one a ferry trip away; we were immersed in the busy life all this entailed. We didn't have time for a dog that needed extra attention, and didn't have money for a dog who needed constant medical or behavioural care, but we had always had dogs in our lives and a year without one had seemed oddly incomplete, not to mention that deer regularly came in the early hours to browse our roses and tender greens, to nip the tops off the raspberry canes and shoots of anything succulent.

When I first saw her, she was lying on the ground, tied by a rope to a scrubby cedar. A man met me at the truck and said, "That's the dog, that's Lady." As I moved towards her, I was already planning my excuse. She looked thin and unkempt, her hips jutting out. Her coat was very black. There was something about her that spoke of the wild, not needy and cuddly the way dogs so often are, and not quite domesticated. The man explained that a few families had shared her and one of the families was moving to Vancouver; the other family didn't want sole responsibility for her care. As I approached her, she rolled onto her back in complete submission, as if she expected to be kicked. There was a smell of old excrement, as though she was living in her own waste. I reached down to pat her and she licked my hand, her eyes meeting my eyes. What I saw there was recognition; we knew each other. I didn't know about perfect but I knew I had to take her home with me.

The first thing we noticed about her was that she'd never been on stairs before. Our house is surrounded by decks of varying sizes and heights and to get to any door you go up a course of stairs. She was so awkward on the stairs that we all had to laugh. She was long-legged and high-hipped, a long-stemmed wildflower. Lady didn't suit her but Lily did. She knew her name as soon as we used it.

From the start we'd decided she'd live outside. Our other dogs had been inside at night but with the children all around and the woodstove in the middle of the kitchen where we spent most of our time, we couldn't imagine a young dog in among it all, especially one the size of Lily, bumping into children and maybe knocking them against the airtight. Our old dog had become incontinent and I'd wake in the morning and come downstairs to find urine all over the floor. Washing the floor before anything else, even coffee, was the way I'd begin the long day, often with a baby waiting to be nursed and a fire needing to be lit. So outside, then, but that was what Lily had been used to. Her previous owners had never had her in their houses. The cedar tree had been her shelter. John began to build her a house and once, pausing after he'd finished nailing plywood to joists for the floor, he noticed her step up onto the platform, certain of ownership. He finished the walls, insulating them and putting cedar siding, left over from our house, on the exterior and a shake roof over it all. An old blanket inside, a picture drawn by one of the children hanging over the entrance. She'd lie in her house like a queen, her paws crossed over the threshold.

Occasionally we'd find odd things inside. A bone, a scrappy bit of stick. Once my daughter came running to say that a squirrel was sleeping in Lily's house. It wasn't sleeping, it was dead and stiff, and Lily wasn't very happy when we removed it. When she was young, she was quite an agile hunter, taking rabbits mid-leap and once, a grouse. The children were upset with her but we tried to tell them how it was a remarkable thing that her hunting instinct was still strong and to notice how proud she was to have provided meat.

She went everywhere with us — down to the lake for our daily swim in summer, in our little boat to find quiet places for picnics. She'd stand at the prow, eager to be the first to jump onto the rocks of White Pine Island. She wasn't really a water dog, despite her Labrador blood, but she liked to have a quiet paddle, away from the humans, and she liked to stand up to her ankles in the lake and drink deeply. She always preferred to drink wild water — the lakes, mountain streams on our hikes, rivers like the Chilcotin, the Blackwater, Kispiox, the Nicola, pausing to sniff the messages coming down from warm hills or across ancient forests. She'd choose puddles or the reedy water of our small pond over clear well water in a bowl. I'd never had a dog before who seemed so connected to its wild origins; there was, in Lily, a dignified refusal to be trained or managed. She would be part of our pack but on her own terms. Some of this was clarified when a man from the Sechelt Indian Reserve came to buy our old brown truck. He recognized Lily right away, only using her old name Lady, and asked if we knew she was part wolf. We hadn't known, but in a way it explained aspects of her character and her physiology, not quite Labrador or Shepherd. And later, seeing a television program on the Kermode bears of Princess Royal Island, I was fascinated to see the packs of black wolves on the island. I'd known that there were black phases in many wolf populations but seeing these wolves, with Lily sleeping just outside, was like looking at her family photographs. The same hips, sharp flanks, the intelligent eyes and the shape of the face.

Because of her, I saw more of the world than I might have otherwise. Daily we'd walk the woods around our home, stopping on the trail to look at bobcat droppings, dead mice, owl pellets, piles of tarry bear scat, watching startled grouse rise as we passed. She noticed everything, sniffing and marking. At Haskins Creek, which runs into the lake near our place, and where we walked three or four times a week, I'd hold Lily's collar while we watched coho salmon making their way up the swift water to spawn in the gravel. Her nose worked in the cold air, taking in the scent of salmon, of bears who'd dragged the carcasses onto the banks, the eagles who waited in the tall cedars. I wondered what she felt as she stood with me there. I know she'd have preferred to be free to find a carcass to roll in — and certainly she found a lot of those, coming back with a proud step, rotting fish caked into her shoulders — but I felt in those moments as though we were all one organism; looking at the deep green and burgundy and steel-grey fish under the water was like peering into a scrying glass and seeing my soul. In Lily's eyes, I saw my own self reflected back, increasingly so as she grew older and her eyes took on the deep blue of old mirror glass. I wanted to have her clear sense of smell, to know what she knew as she found something interesting on a thread of scent, to lift my head as she did and follow the trail of danger or exhilaration.

We acquired a second dog when Lily was ten, reasoning that she could train it to keep deer away and help her with her other duties. She was beginning to stiffen up with the arthritis that crippled her at the end and we hoped that a young dog would keep her moving, keep her agile. The new dog, Tiger, a retriever cross, adored her at first sight. Lily's reciprocal affection was longer in developing but she was patient and tolerant of a puppy's energy and enthusiasm. They had a game we called playing wolves, where Tiger would lie on the ground and Lily would rough her up, teeth bared, hackles up, and a low growl coming up from her throat with a convincing tone of menace to it. When we walked them, the game would be played at a particular point on the route, Tiger beside herself with excitement as she anticipated the moment when Lily would begin the game. It was interesting to watch because so much of it resembled wolf behaviour we'd seen on nature shows or read about. Even their marking was a thread that linked them to their ancestors. When I peed on the trail they'd wait politely for me to get up and then they'd pee over top. Particular spots were peed on daily. I've read that members of a pack mark to indicate to others within the pack certain details of fertility, health, movement, food supply and so on. I've wondered, since Lily's death, what she was telling us in the days of her last walks as she awkwardly peed on an old stump, a new fallen tree. She'd been spayed before we got her but could she smell my own fertility and was she deferring to me as a dominant female? Was she telling us that her heart was weak, that her hips were becoming paralyzed, that she no longer knew where her limbs were in space? Was this her way to prepare us for loss?

I've read that female wolves who don't have a litter help the other females with the business of looking after the young. They bring food to regurgitate for the pups, help watch them while the mother goes for food for herself. I thought of this often, watching Lily and Tiger. Tiger came to us a tiny pup and Lily groomed her, barked curious messages to her that resulted in changed movement or activity, and Tiger would lick Lily's mouth rapidly, hoping for regurgitated food, although she had her own feeding bowl and received special puppy food. And Lily could always be found where the children were, not necessarily part of their activity but keeping an eye on them. Once, over a Christmas season, when the children were inside with me, I put on a record of Dylan Thomas reading "A Child's Christmas in Wales", keeping the volume high so I could hear it while I worked in another room. Outside, Lily became very distressed, hearing an unknown voice booming inside, and I had to calm her, assure her we were alright, and then turn the volume down.

Although so much of our lives overlapped, there were times when the dogs surprised me with their privacy, their otherness. Lily occasionally howled for no apparent reason. And the two dogs would race into the woods, barking in full voice, coming back after a time with their eyes shining and an air of secrecy surrounding them. Sometimes their days were like windows: once, driving up the highway, I came across both dogs on a grassy verge, about a mile from our house, Lily gnawing on a deer leg a hunter had cut off his trophy and cast aside, and Tiger waiting patiently for her to finish so that she could have a share, while around them ravens croaked in the trees, waiting, too.

When I stopped to send them home, it was like I'd interrupted a moment brought forward from their deep history.

Lily took her jobs seriously, keeping deer away from the garden, treeing raccoons who'd come in the fall looking for shelter to hole up in for the winter, chasing bears. The fall before she died, there was a bear, a big male, who began hanging around our place. He didn't want the fruit from the orchard (another bear came for the pears) or vegetables from the garden, but garbage. His visits began the night after a party where we'd barbequed a number of sockeye salmon and put the foil in the garbage cans in a bin. He took the cans away down the bank and went through them, selecting the foil and other wrappers smelling of meat. Even though we began to store the cans in a shed, he still hung around. It was eerie to come back from a walk and see him shambling down the bluffs in front of the house, knowing that he'd waited for us to leave before looking around for garbage. Catching his scent on the wind, Lily would bellow and give chase. She was so stiff with arthritis that she had trouble getting up and lying down but she didn't hesitate to charge at the bear, chasing him until she'd judged he was far enough away; she'd come back to us, walking slowly, panting but proud. She'd bark all night if he was around and was magnificent in her courage. One evening we were packing up the truck to go off for a weekend camping trip and he came up the driveway, swaying and clacking his teeth aggressively. Lily made certain she was between us and him and used a voice I'd never heard before, fierce and wild. It kept him at bay but we realized that he was going to be a constant problem and had the conservation officer live-trap him to take him away over the mountain.

Lily's last weeks were difficult. Most days she couldn't get up on her own, despite pain-killers and anti-inflammatories. We'd lift her from her bed in the woodshed (we'd put her bedding there so she could be seen from the kitchen window) and help her stumble out to a patch of sunlight on the driveway or lawn. She was incontinent, so I'd bring a bowl of warm water and wash her hind legs and tail. She liked the attention but was confused about her legs. We'd move her again after a few hours, lifting her up and encouraging her to walk to keep her legs from swelling, which they had begun to do as a result of edema. Her bedding would need washing and I'd bring out clean towels and old sheets for her to lie on. What she liked best was to eat a bowl of tinned food — her usual diet had been dry food — and then have her ears and head gently stroked. Tiger was puzzled and wondered why Lily wouldn't play. She'd lick Lily's face, her mouth, try to get her up by biting at her hind legs, pulling her tail. Then she'd lie somewhere near, watching the washing, the stroking.

The prerogative to make a decision to end a life is a difficult privilege. There are so many things to consider: whether you are doing it for the animal's sake, your own, whether it might be best to let nature take its own slow course. But there's a time when an animal loses its essence, the sacred element integral to its being: for Lily, not being able to run, to even walk slowly through her woods and cause the grouse to rise, to move from place to place of her volition, seemed to cause her confusion. It distressed her to pee on her bedding and she'd try to clean it up herself. When she had a bowel movement and we weren't there to move her, she would somehow inch her hind end away, obviously with terrible effort. We made an appointment with the vet and told the children to say their goodbyes to her. For our daughter, there was no memory before her. Every camping trip had included Lily, every season. They were nearly the same age. For our middle son, she had come when he was three. His memory of the previous dog faded, although for some months after that one had died, he said he could hear her barking underground. Our oldest son was away at school and we phoned him to tell him of the decision. He wept, for Lily certainly, but also for the passing away of the long years of childhood, anchored as they were by hearth and home, a black dog waiting at the top of the hill for children coming home from school.

I rode to the vet in the back canopy of our truck because I knew Lily didn't have the ability to brace herself against the turns in the winding road south. I'd made her a nest of soft blankets and carried a jug of water to pour out into her dented steel bowl. I wish I'd thought to collect water from a favourite stream although how would I choose? I see her now, up to her ankles in the Chilcotin, the Blackwater, Kispiox, Nicola or the familiar waters of Haskins Creek, smelling of ripe coho and melting snow off the mountains. The vet came out to the truck and gently examined her, listened to her heart. It was very weak. For the ride down, she had given her strength over to me; I held her and it was like holding a warm pelt, smelling musky and wild. When the vet listened to her heart, she leaned more heavily into me. But she didn't object to his presence, she was mild as ever. He brought out a hypodermic of euthanol and said it would happen very quickly. I held my hand over her eyes. "Don't look," I told her, "You don't want to see this." She was so calm. After he removed the needle from her foreleg, I put my face to hers to kiss her goodbye. In her lovely eye, I saw light disappear, literally extinguish like a tiny flame, her life simply fading away until it was like looking into space, where the deep blue of her eye held stars, a whirling cosmos, but no longer her or me. Whatever was once Lily had gone into the thin air around us. There ought to be words for that moment: *Who hath put wisdom in the inward parts? or who hath given understanding to the heart?* And yet words are too few and too many.

After we'd laid her to rest in our woods, I saw her for days afterwards, lying in a shadow of tree, partly hidden by shade. A trick of the eye, of habit — years of seeing unwilling to allow absence. I'd be doing something inside and I'd think, "I'd better go move Lily." Or look for her pan to give her a little meal. I knew what it must feel like to lose a limb and then reach for it, unthinking, or wake to the moment before memory reminds us of loss. Tiger slept in a tight ball in the last place Lily lay before we lifted her into the truck; she kept to that spot for some days afterwards.

There were days when Lily dreamed, as she slept, of running. Days when her stiff legs and crippled hips were young again. We could see her feet racing as she slept, heard her yip with pleasure as she ran, racing with her older family far away, maybe up a long inlet or vast island with salmon and deer and white bears. Running to meet us in the future, waiting on our hill.

∾

Drunkard's Path

THE FIRST DRUNKARD'S Path quilt that I saw was in Provo, Utah, on New Year's Day, 1990. We'd been walking the wide deserted street of the old town, lined with graceful brick storefronts, and had paused in front of a shop called Lizzy Thorne's. It was the first place to really intrigue me in Provo. Everything else so far had been a disappointment — the University where my husband would be working, but which seemed to be little more than a bible college (posters everywhere for revivals and appropriate verses in the most unlikely places), the dingy apartment which had been arranged for us with its chipped iron bedsteads and shabby couch, and the endless stretch of fast food restaurants and chain stores that can be found anywhere in urban North America. I had somehow expected a mountainy town full of gracious houses (we had yet to find them though they existed) — the air full of ideas and student excitement.

The windows in Lizzy Thorne's shop were hung with twiggy wreaths and show-cased Victorian pottery; in one window, an astonishing yellow and white quilt was displayed across a big bed framed with pine logs. I didn't know it was a Drunkard's Path until a few days later when I saw a similar pattern in a quilting book at the Provo public library. At that point I was a new quilter; I'd made two from my own designs, and was figuring out how to do things more or less as I went along. I hadn't expected to love quilt-making so well when I began, but I'd always been attracted to fabric, and thought a lot about textiles in women's lives. For centuries, women made art of practical and everyday items — tablecloths and cushion covers, for instance. Blankets woven from wool gathered from a family's herd or from linen spun from flax, coloured with plant-dyes and homely pigments extracted from iron nails or urine. A piece of knitting might well be a narrative in its own right, patterns and cables telling a story as intimate as a letter. At baby showers I'd noticed how women held the small sweaters and nightgowns to their cheeks, lovingly, before handing them around the circle. Some smelled them, others closed their eyes.

I wasn't sure I understood the stitching part properly and this was why I'd looked for quilting books at the library. I had an idea that the exquisite stitching in the really beautiful examples I'd seen in museums and shops was not entirely necessary for me. I could outline squares or shapes with plain stitching and still have something durable and beautiful. It seemed to me that the really close needlework had been necessary when the layer sandwiched between the quilt top and backing was the traditional cotton batting which came apart so easily. The newer spun battings were stronger and I hoped it would be all right to leave larger gaps between the stitches. I turned out to be reasonably correct, though the books stressed the joy of fine stitching and offered many examples that would have caused me to quietly give up if I hadn't been living in Provo.

Being in Provo made us feel for the first time that our lives were conspicuously different from the lives of those around us. Many of the things we did, no one else did. We drank coffee, for instance, but drinking coffee and buying coffee were not among the cultural habits of the Mormons in Provo. We arrived without a filter basket for our coffee thermos and I thought it would be easy to pick one up at the local supermarket when I went to buy a pound or two of French roast. There turned out to be only one store in Provo — population 85,000 — that sold real coffee. For a few days, until I found this store, we'd take our thermos to McDonalds to have it filled. Usually the coffee had to be made first. The menu listed it, along with Postum, but no one ordered it except those passing through and, as it turned out, us.

And we didn't go to church — in a town where life revolves around churches. There were churches every few blocks; and the Temple, which serves a slightly different function but no one would tell what it was, exactly, was right behind our apartment house. People going to the Temple would park in front of our place, take suitcases from the trunks of their cars, and carry them in. Many things that people did in the course of their days had to do with church, either directly or indirectly. On Sundays, they all attended at least once, and on other days they took their children to church-run day care or went to cookery classes run by the women of their church, or they met with others of their church and discussed relationships, emergency preparedness, scripture. Although our neighbours were friendly and brought cookies to welcome us, we were so obviously not of them and our children were clearly not of them as well. Eventually we learned to drive away on Sundays, to find interesting places to hike or explore. Once we found a town tucked up in the mountains where we drank beer and ate Texas barbeque. And I took to closing the drapes in our front room because I felt uncomfortable at the steady stream of people passing on their way to classes or the laundry room or to information sessions on how to keep a marriage alive. I wanted to drink coffee and look at quilt patterns without being watched or cheerfully waved at.

The choice of fabric in Provo was extraordinary. Every block had a shop, there were cottons galore, not just a small section of them as I was accustomed to, and every bolt cried out for quilts. It was a kind of drunkenness being in those shops, stroking the soft cloth and smelling the keen odours of starch and sizing. I bought masses of fabric — soft blue prints, butter yellow cotton with little slubs of uneven weaving, old-fashioned calico, bright clashing pinks and purples, yards of unbleached muslin, chambray, pinwale corduroy that felt like velvet. I'd no idea what I'd make, no idea how much of anything I'd need. I just amassed stuff, folded it into a red plastic laundry basket, and let it wait. And a further drunkenness, plunging my arms deep into the basket and feeling the bundles of cloth against my arms like sleeves.

And we drank "alcohol". No one else in Provo drank, at least no one we met admitted to drinking. The University (our landlord) included specific injunctions against alcohol in its tenancy agreement. Provo was, after all, the Mormon equivalent of the Vatican with its Temple and church-sponsored University.

But we liked wine and we had expected to find some of those great California wines that you can't get in Canada.

To get to the liquor store you had to drive way down Freedom Boulevard, as though you were leaving Provo, keeping an eye out on the right for a small cinderblock building with iron bars on the windows and door, an unpaved parking lot, and a small man sprinkling salt on the icy sidewalk in front. It was always the same man. He had, what seemed to me, a knowing little smile on his face. Either we were breaking the rules by walking into the store to buy wine or else we were Gentiles. Casual Mormons tended not to live in Provo. We heard from several people that cultural habits were more relaxed in the ranching country in the south-eastern part of the State and that people there drank beer regularly and kept a coffee pot warm on the back of the stove. We never met these free spirits ourselves, but did find that we could get a glass of wine with our meal in restaurants in Moab or Salt Lake City, even if the other diners were drinking root-beer floats with their prime-rib. Sometimes I'd pass the liquor store on my way to buy fabric and I'd see the man sprinkling salt so that the drinkers wouldn't stumble on their way in or out, smiling his knowing smile.

Sometimes I'd go down to the main street and stand in front of Lizzy Thorne's shop to look at the Drunkard's Path. I loved the bright yellow and white, glowing against the pine frame of the bed. It wasn't quite like the Drunkard's Paths in the quilting books. The pieces of this one were straight-edged while the ones in the books were curved. Either way, pieced together, they formed blocks and then the blocks were sewn together to make the path. What intrigued me was the variety of presentation. For one early seamstress, whose sample was pictured in a book, the path had been formally determined; the route that the drunkard had to follow was clearly established and remained constant throughout the quilt. For another, there was no rhyme nor reason to the piecework; the blocks gave a whimsical and riotous impression of a drinker far into his cups aimlessly wandering and coming up against the barrier of another block, or transferring from a path made of light pieces to a path composed of dark cotton. The Drunkard's Path in Lizzy Thorne's was formally designed, but the pattern seemed simpler for a beginner because the triangles and squares would be easier to sew together than circles and curves. One day I went into the shop and stood by the bed and ran my fingertips over the lovely quilt, feeling the soft ancient cotton and the texture of the stitching. Someone else, a woman almost certainly, had planned that bedcover, spent hours charting the pattern, counting the number of squares and triangles she'd need, storing muslin for the back, perhaps even carefully unpicking sugar sacks (for the back was pieced together with rectangles of slightly coarsely woven cloth) and measuring endlessly, making do. I wondered if she waited, as I did, until the children were in bed before taking up her frame. (I used a lap-hoop but many women had frames in which to stretch their quilts for stitching. These could be lowered from the ceiling by means of a pulley or else folded up and stored away. I kept my quilts folded in a large basket beside the couch so that I could get them immediately when I found myself with spare time.) I liked her simple colour scheme, which seemed to show a sweet tolerance of drunkenness. Some Drunkard's Paths that I'd seen in the library books had been devised of busy prints, or stark white and navy blue, and even one in an ironic burgundy and green, for the morning after.

One Sunday we drove up past Sundance and the Reservoir to Heber City. On the map, it looked to be a decent-sized place but in fact there was just one main street of shops, churches of course, and a couple of fast-food restaurants. A little collection of shops was clustered around a ticket office for the steam train that made scenic tours of the mountains in good weather and in one of these shops, a woman was busy stitching together the ugliest quilt-tops I'd ever seen. She was an excellent needle-woman, her stitches small and even, but the fabrics she used were ill-matched and lurid. She seemed to have no overall idea of colour or harmony or even intention; she simply made up blocks of whatever was available and then made tops of them without any apparent meditation. A great pile of the completed tops, ready for matching up with batting and backing, were for sale, priced cheaply. And there were a few finished quilts, too, showing that marvellous needlework, but I couldn't find one that appealed to me in any way at all. She told me she'd be lost without a quilt to put together and I told her I felt the same way. She was delighted to talk about quilting and kept reaching for work to show me — a Monkey Wrench in mustard yellow and purple, an Irish Chain in nasty prints. We left Heber City and I couldn't help but wonder if she ever looked outside at the dark mountains against an intense blue sky, saw the possibilities of design in the fields surrounding her city — tan and golden and soft green, crisscrossed by irrigation roads.

Imagine a woman's desire to make a first quilt, having admired them in the houses of others or in books. Perhaps she'd moved to a new place and discovered a quilter's guild, a group of women meeting regularly to sit in a circle of flying hands. Perhaps she'd felt a need, as strong as hunger, to make something of beauty to take her out of her life for some time each day, or more deeply into it. One day I was cleaning out a closet at home on the Sechelt Peninsula and had come upon a box of fabric scraps — a piece of polished upholstery cotton left from making new covers for the dining room chairs, a length of corduroy for cushions that never got started, a small piece of velvet from my husband's grandmother's drapes in England, a skirt that hadn't worked out. As I sorted and folded the contents of the box, I saw a quilt emerging out of the cloth, saw the lovely harmonies of blue and tan and rose-beige, and began right then to cut out squares which I pieced together as fast as I cut them. I felt in the heat of creation as I sewed those lopsided squares (for I hadn't known then of templates) and for some weeks after, I saw the possibility of quilts in everything: sunsets, trees against a sky as blue as in a Maxfield Parrish painting, tulips in a cloud of forget-me-nots.

We began to think of our wine bottles as slightly shameful, tucked in behind the fridge. We drank the wine out of little juice glasses as there was nowhere to buy proper wine glasses. We kept telling the children that we believed wine was a civilizing thing, an element of *dining* as opposed to eating, but there at that arborite table, among the cheap dishes and mismatched cutlery, our words sounded a little too defensive. And maybe even desperate. From that great distance, of miles and culture, away from all we knew, our dinner tableaux reminded us of our minority status, our isolation.

In Provo, I thought for the first time in years of the small crib quilt my grandmother had made for my older brother.

Nothing of the sort had been made for me but the little quilt had somehow ended up in my possession. I used it for my children when they were babies, its rough squares of old cotton — remnants of curtains, housedresses, my grandfather's pyjamas — offering a comfort beyond warmth. I didn't know my grandmother very well; she died when I was nine or ten. When she was alive, we visited in the summers and I found her to be rather terrifying — an ancient Slavik-accented matriarch who was practically deaf and lived surrounded by daughters and grandchildren and great-grandchildren, seated in a yellow rocking chair on a porch of a house in Edmonton, far from our home. I looked, all the years later, at the crib-quilt she'd stitched and knew something of her hands, the way she saw colour, the thrifty spirit that must have been so pleased to find a use for the bits of good cloth. The quilt was backed with red and white ticking, perhaps left over from stuffing mattresses with goose feathers from the fowl kept by my grandparents in the days of my father's childhood. It was obvious that my grandmother was not an accomplished quilter; her squares were lopsided and the stitching irregular; but I felt kinship with her in a way more profound than I ever felt sitting by the yellow rocker and trying to decipher what she was saying to me, all those years ago, in summer.

Why did the Drunkard's Path end up in an antique store in Provo? I couldn't imagine why a family member wouldn't treasure its lovely pattern and pass it along, in turn, to a new generation to love and cherish. What's more, I couldn't imagine *buying* the quilt, feeling, I suppose, that I wasn't entitled to such a personal piece of someone else's family history. In a way, the quilt served as a talisman for my days in Provo, a gentle reminder of tolerance and diversity. Drinking a glass of wine at night behind closed drapes, I'd look through the quilt books, hoping to find a pattern for a Drunkard's Path which would match my skills, and catching the poetry in quilting pattern names — Flying Geese, Lone Pine, Double Wedding Ring, Shadows and Light. I wanted to think about the unknown women who stitched such poetry, some by candlelight, some in isolation, poverty, some in a sweet sisterhood (the Friendship quilts moved me to tears). My red basket of cotton sat beside the couch with such secrets hidden in its depths. I made two quilts those months in Provo, an old-fashioned Ohio Star of unbleached muslin and light blue prints, and a dark blue quilt of my own design, decorated with pink and purple chevrons inspired by the hot air balloons which floated over our apartment each Saturday. I kept the Ohio Star to pass down to my daughter one day and gave the dark blue to a friend. I have yet to make a Drunkard's Path, and don't know if I ever will — blues, bottle green, a meandering path through the Sunday roads of Utah.

❧

ERASING THE MAPS

"TWO KILOMETRES FROM Coalmont," I said, reading the information in a travel guide we carried on the trip through British Columbia's southern interior. Coalmont is on the Tulameen Stage Road, leading from Princeton to Aspen Grove through grasslands and ponderosa pines, cliffs of red ochre; the Tulameen River a pretty sight from the heights the road climbs beyond Princeton. We'd just finished a beer at the Coalmont Hotel, the only other customer a man called Bert Sharkey who gave us his business card — *Key Shar Horse Motel: A rustic vacation spot for you & your horse. When you see it you'll wonder why you came. When you leave you'll wonder why you left.* — and encouraged us to drop in the next time we were in the wilderness near the Otter Valley. He had no power and no phone but promised hot showers and two Standardbred horses. When I asked him about Granite Creek, supposedly two kilometres from Coalmont, he said he'd chased cattle through there in years past but hadn't been near the place in ages. On our way out of the hotel, I stopped to look at photographs on the wall by the bathrooms. Several showed motorcycle gangs outside

the hotel. There was also a calendar from 1915, with Coalmont
Hotel printed prominently on the top, but the photograph on
it was captioned, "Scotland by the Sea", with gambolling sheep
on a cliff above a turbulent ocean. An old newspaper clipping,
framed, reported the opening of the hotel in 1912 with a High
Mass to celebrate. A lovely old dog, grey-faced and smelly, was
sleeping on the verandah as we left and wagged its tail as we
leaned over to pat it. Crossing the road to our car, I heard violent
and tubercular coughing and spitting which I assumed was the
dog, until I turned and saw a second-storey door closing on the
hotel's narrow balcony. We had wondered about permanent
residents. Now we had our answer.

We wanted to see what might be left of Granite Creek,
founded in 1885 when Johnny Chance struck it rich by finding
gold in the waters of the creek itself; by 1887 it was the third
largest community in British Columbia. We drove over the
bridge across the Tulameen River, turned left, and made our
way along a gravel road. There was a grassy open area where
the road began to climb up towards Blakeburn, a single ruined
cabin calm in its centre, but the distance was well short of two
kilometres so we kept driving. Up the road, past the sign for
the Granite Creek Cemetery which we intended to explore
after we'd found Granite Creek itself, a sign announced the
presence of logging trucks on the gravel road and offered a
radio frequency for those with the equipment to monitor such
things. We were in our small silver Toyota and the road was
narrow; we didn't want to meet a huge truck careening around
one of the blind corners. Well past two kilometres we decided
that Granite Creek didn't want to be found, so we went back to

the Cemetery and explored the high shelf where pickets, bare and some newly painted, corralled the dead.

A shop in Princeton held racks of postcards showing old views of the area. I studied them and bought one, circa 1895, showing Granite Creek at full water, a cluster of cabins and what appeared to be a flume; remnants of snow could be seen on the trail leading down from the photographer's perch. I knew from reading whatever I could find on the area that a man called Foxcrowle Percival Cook had been a storekeeper at Granite Creek and I was intrigued to find his grave, alongside the grave of his four-year-old daughter Frances Mary Cook. I was to learn later from looking at Birth and Death records that his wife Emma was buried at Princeton almost forty years later. The ground in the Granite Creek Cemetery was strangely uneven, the shapes of graves sunk into soil but there were no markers, no borders of neat pebbles. There were recent burials, some in the 1990s, so it was still a place alive enough in memory for people to want to be put into its earth, among the pine trees and wild roses. Rhodes, McBride, Lucas; and William D. Morrison, with his poignant inscription, "No More Trials or Pain." So many of the markers had worn beyond legibility with age and weather, but among the few still clear enough to read was the one for Charlie and Nellie Blank, their names on a simple picket stake with a heart etched into the old wood.

When we got to the bottom of the road, we noticed the sign which we'd thought had pointed up the road but in fact indicated the open area with the cabin. We quickly realized that the travel book had been overly generous in its estimate of distance and that this was Granite Creek, where the smooth-rocked tributary met the Tulameen River. The cabin was tarped in blue, with a sign saying that it was being restored by a heritage group and that the work would be completed in 2001. It was then June of 2003. A few other foundations had gone to ground, one holding two walls which were nearly completely collapsed. There were two apple trees which didn't look particularly old, but apparently the last four residents of Granite Creek stayed until the mid 1950s; these might have been later plantings. The trees were heavy with pale pink bloom and I could also see lots of gooseberry bushes. There were old lilacs around areas that might have been entrances to houses or to one of the thirteen saloons which supplied miners with refreshment and consolation. There had been a fire in 1907 which pretty much destroyed most of the town, but even after gold fever had died down, people continued to make a living, supporting a store for a time, and no doubt some sort of drinking establishment. In a pit, which we thought might be a well or a grey water area (where sinks would have drained in the absence of septic tanks), which was lined with river stones, a mouse huddled on the dry bottom, shaking in fear. When we left to get a rough shake for it to use as a plank to escape, it disappeared into some tunnels among the rocks.

Where had Foxcrowle Percival Cook's store been located? One account of the community says that the fire began there. But the store was rebuilt and later relocated to Coalmont in 1912. And where had his children played? Adelaine, Emily, Frances (the poor one sharing her father's gravesite, though twenty years before him alone in the earth), Eda, Agnes, and Edward: children growing like young trees on the banks of the Tulameen River. I like to think that they brightened the lives of miners long absent from their own families, provided charming details for letters written to remote corners of the earth. What did they think about the shooting, of which I've read there was plenty. The knives, the horses, the "temples of Bacchus"? Their father died in 1918, in Vancouver, and I wonder whether it was the Spanish influenza that took him, and whether he returned to Granite Creek by train, a sad passenger in a coffin, placed among the freight and sacks of mail.

There are almost no clear echoes in Granite Creek — of voices of long-ago children, or clamour of stories in the tall grass. It is a place of deep absence, absence in the remnants of cabins, hand-hewn logs fitting together in the corners like lovers. The trees contain nothing, not even nests of magpies whose great-parents might have greeted the morning like a raucous gang. And yet we linger for a time, walking the perimeter where cars have stopped, where rings of stones have been created for campfires and where beer cans have been shot at, then left to glint like silver in the grass. I stand still and close my eyes briefly, hoping to hear something, *anything*, but there are only bees humming in wild roses and yarrow. A grasshopper clicks in the grass. But I am discovering there are echoes, and echoes. Some, not clear nor immediate, insinuate themselves into the imagination, the heart, and make their small noise long after the sound has stopped. A resonance, a whisper — voices or a phrase of music carrying on after silence.

I dream of the storekeeper's children a week later, wondering if there had been a school in Granite Creek for them. I can find no record though nearby Coalmont had one later on. There was no church in the early years either, and services were held once a month by the Reverend George Murray in private homes or else in one of the hotels. I dream of the children in sunlight, eyes full of weather, the knowledge of specific pines, hands stained with dandelions. Vital Statistics holds records of their births, deaths, marriages, and somewhere there would be records of land grants and holdings. Foxcrowle and Emma were married in Lower Nicola, I discover, one of my favourite places on earth. I could make family trees, and map out the townsite, and even make a grid of its physical appearance. But what is lost here, at least to me, is the shape of a place, known and held in memory, loved well enough that those dying a century later would desire its earth. The echo of these children will sound itself in odd ways — a name, pondered like a wishing stone; a website of a family, listing antecedents; a photograph showing a clearing with some cabins, snow, a declaration of trails on the mountain above.

On my desk is a fragment of embossed tin ceiling tile, found in the grass where it was rusting away. I thought twice about taking it home with me, wondered if the act would be considered theft or grave-robbing, but the fragment was flaky and not long for this world and I knew I'd look at it daily, feeling a shiver as I thought of its provenance. Had it been painted? Had it graced the ceiling of a hotel or saloon? Objects wait all over the landscape with their fading narratives of settlement and loss. I hunted down maps from various sources to look at how Granite Creek was represented during its heyday and long decline — the bold type, or faint. I found it on the CPR map of 1893 and a Rand McNally map of 1896; but by 1914, the CNR map (released a year before the trains were actually running on its tracks) showed only the geographical feature of the creek and didn't indicate a town. I ran a search on the Provincial Archives site and got some photographs, citations for

Provincial Police correspondence, government agent records, but no cartographic references.

At what point is a place simply erased from a map in its very literal sense? All over British Columbia there are significant town sites which hold only ghosts of their former selves. As a young woman I hiked to Leechtown on Vancouver Island and remember the decaying cabins, the occasional iron pot, a trailing run of fence. There is almost nothing left there now. Cemeteries can anchor a name but what of those who lie outside? Addresses on old envelopes call to mind a residence, a street or post-office long returned to forest or field. Plants last far longer than buildings sometimes, the buildings easily taken apart and reconstructed elsewhere, but roots and seeds have a lingering affinity with their earth. I think of the delphiniums at Barkerville, the gold-rush town site west of Quesnel, now a Provincial Heritage Site. There are common lilacs, even in the fenced-off areas around the few remaining buildings still in private hands, and thus not tended by park contractors or teams of volunteers. Not far from Barkerville, old buildings sit in clearings at Stanley, Lightning Creek, Beaver Pass — all busy towns in the gold-rush period. There is the faint impression of a race track at nearby Antler where horse races were held — hot blooded horses having been imported from England in 1861 and brought up what was then the Cariboo Trail — and where Governor Douglas attended a meet prior to the construction of the Cariboo Road. And yet where is Antler on the maps? I suppose ghosts (*those unmarked graves*), the remnants of a race track, the standing chimney of a house long abandoned, are not solid enough evidence of occupation and industry for cartographers to keep pencilling in the names on new maps. Still they have their own resilience.

Later, I read Don Blake's book on Blakeburn, which was the coal mining camp on the mountain above Granite Creek which flourished from the 1920s until the 40s. I learn that following the mine explosion on August 13, 1930, a day known as Black Wednesday for the forty-five men who perished, graves were dug at the Granite Creek cemetery for the bodies recovered after the explosion. A few men were buried there but most were transferred to Princeton or even Vancouver; the depressions in the ground are memories of those temporarily laid in the earth: the men who perished on Black Wednesday as well as the Chinese workers killed in everyday accidents who were buried temporarily until their bones could be sent back to China. It is hard to know, walking over uneven ground, whether one walks on a natural depression or a place which still holds the shape of a man taken away.

Bert Sharkey remembered chasing cattle through Granite Creek, suggesting it had been part of a range, a wilderness. Photographs from the 1950s reveal a few cabins still inhabited (smoke in the chimneys, a window opened to the morning). Photographs from the early 1960s focus on detritus, fallen walls, yet earlier photographs offer panoramas of cabins, the two streets (Miners and Government), a house with a garden plot neatly weeded. And in books about ghost towns, side roads and forgotten camps, a map will show the place itself, in bold type, as worthy of our attention as Paris or Vancouver. A road will be described, contours and elevations indicated, and for a moment, what comes alive is nearly everything that ever was — buildings lit by oil lamps, gardens ablaze with flowers, children running from one door to another with smaller children tailing them, mothers hanging out wash and gathering enough gooseberries for a fool, wood being chopped, a storekeeper wiping a counter with a cloth cut from a worn flannel shirt. In a saloon, sawdust is being spread on the floor while whiskey is downed in the blink of an eye. Everything that has happened is happening again. The old dog leaps from the verandah to run the scant kilometre to a clearing where familiar voices have summoned him to sit down, shake a paw. And I wonder if that's why someone still lives in the Coalmont Hotel, waiting for the moment when every ache might vanish, the breathing come easy, the river hasten over rocks as it once did when he was young and found his footing among wild roses and tall grass; when the dead will turn in their graves above Granite Creek and smile to hear magpies again.

Six Stones on a Summer Windowsill

1. Stone House

I dreamed of a stone house by the edge of the last fields. There were horses there and a rumour of cougars in the groves of oaks. No one else could see the house, though I wanted to buy it, inquired about an owner, peered in windows wispy with curtains. The fields were everything I remembered, rich with wildflowers, a new foal, grasses heavy with seed. A man had killed a cougar and brought its entrails in a bucket for everyone to see and nod over, though I could not tell what might be known from the contents of its stomach. I was alone in my confusion. And alone in my quest for that stone house, thick-walled, the fields spread out before it, blooming and sweet-smelling.

2. Walking the Shore Trail

I was a girl alone in Beaver Lake park, walking the shore trail with my dog. It was spring, the air filled with the scent of new leaves, rich earth; and I was walking with a heart filled with loneliness, alone in the world, or so it seemed, although

I had parents and brothers, a few good friends. I was walking, wondering what the future held for me, although I wouldn't have thought this quite so clearly. One minute I was walking; the next I was diving underwater, not myself but something that belonged in the lake, long and sinewy. I had seen an animal out of the corner of my eye perhaps and for a moment I *was* that other life, moving down among the reeds and the mud to emerge, face-first, to watch the lonely girl and her dog on the shore trail. I was not myself but the potential of self, the possibility of joining my being with another, not human, but something wild and possessed with the urgency of living. When I came back into myself, I felt enormous with what had happened and wanted to tell someone. At home, my parents sat at the table and drank instant coffee, their faces closed as toads while I tried to say that I had entered the life of the lake for a brief moment only, knew another way to belong to the earth and its vast complexity of animals and plants, was for a moment the weasel, the otter, the dark-haired swimmer. They turned from me in that moment and I was alone again in the world, with parents, brothers, a few friends only, while the water waited with its secrets, its mysterious reeds.

3. Blue Bathtubs

There were four or five of them, all laid out in a yard somewhere, a builder's yard, a cobbled area, where they were shown to their best advantage, in the air, wind around them, sunlight filling them like water. Each had been restored, the interior porcelain thick and creamy, the exteriors all painted and glazed in the colours of sea-glass — cobalt, rich aqua, sky. They were longer than the one we are currently storing in our carport, its interior chipped and worn, its exterior rusted and flaking its brown paint; these were long enough to recline in, full-length, with white legs stretching out in front and warm water reaching my chin. We had thought to restore the one in our carport, to replace our old tub with it, perched in our bathroom on its elegant clawed feet, its beauty and comfort anticipated as I lay in our rough tub. But it was a little long for the space — though not as long as the blue tubs — and we did not want to knock out walls, make more work for ourselves than necessary. So now it waits for a purpose — it had been used for compost by a gardener no longer weeding with us — and might wait for years yet while we come up with the ideal solution. I see it perhaps tucked in among ferns as a raised pond for our treefrogs to lay their eggs in, a place where the snakes could not reach the tender clusters of salamander eggs, the young tadpoles. But I dreamed of the beautiful blue tubs and woke wishing for something more for my life, my bath hour, the possibility of sinking into the creamy interior where the sunlight has gathered, warming me.

4. Grey Ponies at Gurteen

I wish I could say I was not drunk. But in fact my friend and I had met two young musicians travelling west from Dublin — they picked us up hitchhiking near Oughterard — who passed a bottle of John Jameson back and forth in the small dirty car, and by the time we were at the crossroads, one leading us to the safety of the town where I often stayed on shopping trips away from the island where I then lived, the other road leading to the lights and pubs of Roundstone and the company of these two joyous men, my friend was nudging me and I was nudging her and we were saying, Yes, we'd go with them for the craic. My friend and I helped them to empty the bottle by the time we'd reached Roundstone. By midafternoon we'd had pints of Guinness in one of the pubs, listened to the story of a fisherman who'd been lost on the water for a week and who gave me the pencil he'd kept in his pocket during the ordeal ("Ye're a writer. Ye could use it, I'm thinking."), and then we'd driven the bog road to Clifden where the two musicians joined in a session at the Celtic Bar. It was wild being the girls with the musicians, the girls passing the bodhran over to replace the fiddle, to hand over a pint while the guitar player took a brief break to drink from the glass and then wipe his mouth on the back of his hand. (He was the one I slept with in the B&B later although we shared a bed only, not our bodies; he kept climbing over me to vomit in the sink, his skinny shoulders red with blemishes. His fingers, I remember, had moved over the strings of the guitar like magic.) I wish I could say I'd not been drunk when we decided at midnight to drive out to Gurteen to look at the starlight on the white coral strand but we were over the moon with whiskey, over the moon with old fiddle tunes making me wonder why I'd ever been born in Canada and not Ireland. Would I remember this differently if I'd gone cold sober to that bay on the edge of the world, would I dream of something other than the rocks and the path of silver light leading to the new world? One of the musicians (I don't even recall their names) immediately sank to his knees in the soft sand and cried for his dead mother. My friend held the hand of the one she was going to sleep with that night and walked down the white length. I swayed and wobbled to the grass dunes to look up the peninsula and down, both views possible from the height. And there in the grass were the grey Connemara ponies, two standing, at least two lying down, one walking out of the darkness towards me, body shining, the smell of horse and seaweed and a warm wind touching my cheeks until I cried. I was twenty-two years old and one of the horses came to me, blowing grass-scented air against the hand I held out for it, and stood still as I buried my face in its tangled mane, crying out O God, O God, on the dunes of Gurteen while my musician threw up on the beach and my friend embraced her new love, the Atlantic brushing the sand like kisses.

5. The Life You Might Have Had

You might have lived in your old neighbourhood, on Faithful Street, near the sea, near the Shell Station where your father would stop for gas, butterscotch suckers shaped like shells handed in the car windows to each child in the backseat. Faithful Street, across from the park, where the lovers lanes all lead in to the tangle of snowberry and hazel, where songbirds trill from thickets of broom. On Faithful Street, you might have heard peacocks in the night, you would pass the yellow duplex on Cook Street on walks, the duplex you loved in childhood with its arched gates and pretty windows (so often you dream of Cook Street, the shops of the village, dogs tied to lampposts while the owners buy fish and chips, primulas . . .). Who might your children have been in that life? Would making love in a different room, another bed, curtains falling softly from windows looking out to Clover Point, would that mean that an entirely different family would sit at your table, sleep in beds drawn tight with flowered sheets, would these other children, conceived on Faithful street, have ridden bikes to the park and walked the long avenues with tiny paper bags of jawbreakers, marshmallow bananas? Would you have sent them out for a quart of milk, a loaf of bread, knowing that neighbours would watch out for them, cars stop generously at crosswalks, ghosts of your true children watching from behind a fence, an ornamental cherry? You wonder if they would have imagined somewhere in their long night dreaming, a wooded home not chosen, deer leaving the heart-shaped prints unread on the long walk up.

6. The Dream of the Horse

I'd gone to the basement, to the farthest corner, where the door opens to a crawl space under the stairs. There was a rough fence and behind it, my horse, forgotten all these years. He was lying on soiled straw, the smell of urine strong in the dark corner. A drop of water in one bucket. How could I have forgotten him, I thought, as I cradled his head, how could I have forgotten to feed him, take him out for long rambles on the trail to the lake. His eyes were dull. I promised him everything and filled his water bucket before running upstairs to cry to my parents that I hadn't meant to neglect him, would try harder to be responsible.

Waking, my heart nearly broke with the pain of it. It was so long ago, surely he'd been dead for at least fifteen years, yet I sobbed for my carelessness, the inevitability of my neglect. A horse bought in my girlhood, loved, ridden for miles on trails now long paved over, his bedding turned and changed daily, his water kept clear, his black coat brushed. He went to a new home on an island when I wanted to study further, to travel through Europe, though I thought of him for years, missed the pools of his eyes, the smell of his neck. And in my dark bed, in the depths of a June night, I cried for the inevitable abandonment of all that I loved, all that sustained me through the sad years of my adolescence, my children now gone away from home, my husband embracing my sorrow as surely as he embraces my joy and desire.

∞

MONTH OF WILD BERRIES PICKING

For Charles Lillard & Henry Tate, both wonderful story-tellers, both gone.

December, 1996

LATELY I HAVE been immersed in the ethnology of the Northwest Coast of British Columbia. Collections of Haida songs, Tsimshian tales, views of totems and masks: having travelled a little in the wet air hanging above the Skeena River, having dreamed of driving over the lava beds to the villages of the Nisga'a, planning a trip by boat to Haida Gwaii, I've been reading and looking at whatever comes across my desk. Sometimes a voice speaks out of a book so directly and unexpectedly that I pause, startled. It's like hearing a specific name in the wind's clamour or being overcome by a sudden memory of a mask with separate mouthpieces to articulate a story from several perspectives, maybe a Kwakiutl echo mask, the four mouths hidden away in a pouch until needed. Raven, frog, sea-anemone, bear . . . It's the bear I've been listening for, and hearing when I'm lucky, and it's his story I want to think about here.

One of the books that arrived in the mail from a friend is *The Porcupine Hunter*, a gathering of Tsimshian fables, myths and moral tales (one might call them cautionary tales) written down by Henry Tate from 1903 until his death in 1913. This was a job he had undertaken for Franz Boas and the material formed much of the background for Dr. Boas' own monumental work on the Tsimshian Indians for the Smithsonian Institute's Bureau of American Ethnology. Ralph Maud has transcribed some of Henry Tate's original texts and has gathered them together in a fascinating book where the spirit of Henry Tate, grammatical idiosyncrasies and quirky spellings intact, speaks across the decades to anyone listening.

My favourite tale in the collection is "The History of Kbi'shount" or "The Girl Who Married the Bear". Only one version of a story that is deep in the story-telling consciousness of the Northwest coast as well as inland, among the Tagish and Tutchone, Tate's telling is forceful. It takes place in the time between August and September, *the month*, Tate tells us, *of wild berries picking*. A girl, Half-summer, sister to four hunting brothers, goes berry-picking with the women of her village. She has demonstrated by her carelessness that she is not taking the berry-picking very seriously — her basket keeps breaking, the berries fall to the ground, and the other women are reluctant to assist her after this has happened more than once. She wanders away from them and meets up with a couple of young men.

She told them her line-basket was broke several times. They ask her where is her companion. She can't wait here any longer. Therefore these two men ask her to carry her basket to help her, so she consented. (Tate 33)

Half-summer goes with the young men to a village unknown to her and after a series of incidents involving food, during which Mouse-woman reveals to her the reason for what is now becoming apparent was an abduction — Half-summer had slipped on a pile of bear excrement and had spoken disrespectfully to the pile — the girl becomes the wife of one of the Black Bear chief's sons.

I love the story for what it tells us about girls and authority, about ardour and the capricious nature of the human heart, the mysteries of sexuality, and finally for its insight into interspecies relationships. We have rules in our culture for getting along with each other and all manner of protocol affecting our associations with other humans. But "The Girl Who Married the Bear" reveals the extent to which native stories articulate the complexity and importance of rules that govern relationships between species, a profoundly symbiotic world where one respected not just the territory of another species but its dung, its bones, its very spirit as well.

Sometimes a story speaks to your own experience, your own dream-life, and you attend to it in ways that surprise you. For instance, this past spring a young male black bear was hanging around our woods. We'd seen a mother with a cub just up the mountain the previous year and I wondered if this was the same cub, weaned and sent away to fend for itself. We often have bears pass though our place but they don't stay because of our dogs. This one lingered, too inexperienced to know that the barking of dogs was a sign that he should find territory farther away. Day after day the dogs would race into the woods, bellowing, and every few days when we'd walk the trails, we'd find a new pile of scat, right there in the middle of the trail. He was bold and confident enough to let us know he was around. The scat was firm and large, threaded with grasses and sedges, so I thought he was probably feeding down by Sakinaw Lake in a marshy area where sockeye spawn in December, a place where I wander in spring to collect plants left over from an old homestead now gone into memory.

In "The Girl Who Married a Bear", the girl who is lured away by the bear has slipped on bear excrement. In other versions of the tale, she repeatedly and wilfully kicked at piles of bear scat on the berry-picking outing, something that is taboo in the northern cultures. You can study the droppings to know what the bears have been eating (and thus avoid dangerous areas) but the rules for girls are that you step around the mounds of scat, never over them, and you certainly don't kick at them or tread on them. Half-Summer is angry at slipping on the pile and exclaims, "Oh this big excrement was stick in my foot, alas it very nasty." This sounds like a relatively mild insult, perhaps a momentary lapse of good conduct, but other versions of the tale have the girl wantonly treading on piles of bear dung since childhood, in clear disobedience to the teachings of her mother. In some versions she curses at the bear who has left droppings on the trail:

She got mad at the bear. "Where this dirty bear went out, I fell on it myself!" And she called that bear bad name because of it. And maybe the bear heard it. (McC 16);

and

"What the hell does he defecate for? He goes right around the trail!" That's what she says. She jumps over top of it, and she laughs. (McC 39)

All the versions of the tale that I've read express no surprise that a girl who has displayed such disrespect would be taken by a bear to be its wife.

In the material I've been reading this winter, I've come across all sorts of rules for behaviour during bear encounters. In his wonderful book, *Giving Voice to Bear*, David Rockwell says that among the Koyukon people (from northwestern Alaska), a woman threatened by a bear should expose her genitals and say, "My husband, it's me." This will shame the bear into retreating. (Rockwell 123) The Parks Canada brochure, *You Are In Bear Country*, warns that you should not run or throw anything at a bear encountered while hiking or camping: "If the bear does not seem to be displaying aggressive behaviour, talk softly in monotones and slowly back up. If a bear rears on its hind legs and waves its nose in the air, it is trying to identify you. Remain still and speak in low tones." Both methods are essentially appeals to the bear's good nature, it seems to me, and both acknowledge at least a suggestion of psuedo-humanity implicit or possible in bear behaviour. It is not such a far distance from the initiation rites of many North American Indian tribes in which girls were isolated from their families during menstruation, a time for some when the young women were said to be "going to be a bear", to the directive in the Parks Canada brochure that "women should be extra careful" if camping during menses: "One recommended precaution is the use of tampons which should be disposed of in airtight plastic bags."

The girl who is taken by the bear adapts quite well to her new life, although she still remembers and longs for her brothers. She is happy with her husband, although torn between her human loyalties and her affection for this new family. When she and her new husband are preparing to choose a den for the winter, she keeps warning that her brothers know the den area and that the family bear-hunting dogs know it as well. In the Tate version, this is handled in a particularly evocative way. Wanting to know how effective these bear hunting brothers are in the field, the Black-Bear Chief asks the girl, "Now I'll ask just only one question, is this, How many mats are thy elder brother?" The girl replies, "[M]y elder brother's mats are sixty." (In other words, he is very successful as a hunter of bears.) Then, in a moment of poignant beauty, Tate tells us

> Then sixty Black-Bears
> > bow their heads
> > > and the waters ran down
> on each noses. (Tate 35)

I thought this was a heartbreaking moment because there is no doubt that the bears anticipate their fate; *the waters ran* down *on each noses*. The image of these beautiful animals bowing their heads and crying at the thought of being connected, even through such a curious and irregular marriage, to such consummate hunters had me in tears when I first read this version. Each brother's prowess is described and eventually

> . . . the husband of the Princess
> also bow down his head
> and the water rans down on his nose. (Tate 36)

The moment comes when the chief asks his bears to gather wild carrots to take into their dens for the winter. The old bears announce that they will "lie underneath the olden fallen tree." Winter has arrived.

The rules for living among bears varied from tribe to tribe. Many people believed that bears were very close to humans, too close to be able to eat them with any sort of impunity. In fact, some southwestern tribes thought that bears were simply people without fire; eating them would be cannibalism. Some ate them only when faced with starvation. Some hunted black bears but not grizzlies. Others had highly elaborate rituals that allowed them to placate a bear's spirit and for some the bear was a spirit helper for shamanic ceremonies. James Teit's excellent ethnographic account of the Lillooet tells us that women did not eat bear flesh because to do so would prevent them from having more children or would dissolve any unborn child being carried in the womb.

Some anthropologists have suggested that "The Girl Who Married a Bear" is a teaching story, developed to give a framework for rules associated with bear hunting; the bear gives clear directions to his wife for the treatment of his body, bones, organs and skin once it becomes evident that he is to be killed by the human brothers brought to the den by a variety of devices. In her monograph on the story, Catharine McClellan says that, "His [the bear's] course of action also makes it possible for Indians ever after to cope with the presence of grizzly bears, for he gives explicit instructions how his brothers-in-law should treat his corpse and how peace ceremonies can be carried out between humans and the bears they kill." (McC 8) For me its lessons are also enigmatic, serving to instruct us at a deeply subliminal level in matters of interspecies relationships. It does this by creating an atmosphere that is closer to poetry than to traditional prose narrative. The anthropologist Julie Cruikshank speaks of two domains of narrative in northern aboriginal stories, one being "a historical temporal, secular human world" and the other being "a supernatural, timeless domain which corresponds with 'myth time'". (Cruikshank 21) She stresses the importance of narrative to people's lives, citing examples from her field work among Tagish and Tutchone women where women insisted that particular stories be included in family histories she was helping them to compile. They made little distinction between the quantifiable data of their lives — who was born when, to whom, who married whom, etc. — and the mythic tales of supernatural journeys, marriages with animals, and so on. In fact, the women were emphatic about the necessity of making the stories available to young people as part of school curricula.

In most versions of "The Girl Who Married a Bear", time is distorted as it might be in a dream. In the den the bears sleep for months but, waking, the girl feels as though she has only slept one night. Sometimes the girl remembers her past life and sometimes it is like she dreamed it. There is mystery associated with the campfires and meals; the girl knows the bear makes the fires but they are different, somehow, and he cooks meals of groundhog and gopher but she never sees him doing it. Salmon she has skinned and dried disappear and it seems the bear caches them in his body:

> "He goes this way [reaches into his armpit], and he gives some gophers to his wife. And from this one [indicates the other armpit — the left one(?)], he eats himself. All

kinds of food. King salmon — dry ones too. Blueberries
too. (McC 43)

This story has intrigued me since I first heard it some years
ago, driving the Yellowhead highway with my family between
Hazelton and Terrace. On a stretch where the road followed
the course of the Skeena River, we tuned in a radio station that
was broadcasting a Tsimshian storyteller and "The Girl Who
Married a Bear" was one of the stories told as we drove through
the rain towards Prince Rupert, the powerful words fading out
occasionally as we lost the signal. We saw a number of bears
during that trip, one skidding down the river bank on his rump
to try for sockeye which we'd seen fishermen dip-netting and
gaffing above the narrow chasms at Moricetown. The words of
the storyteller evoked the heat of the den, the closeness of the
bodies, husband, wife and cubs, curled in a dark heap under the
earth. I remember hearing the part about the brothers finding
their sister with her grizzly mate and, later, the intensity of the
moment when she told them they had killed their own brother-
in-law. In the Tate version, we are prepared for the possibility
that the dogs will find Half-summer because of their fondness
for her: "One dog's name was "Red" the other was "spots", and
these two dogs are very lover of the young girl." (Tate 32)

It is a story about deep transformation. The bears burrow
under trees to hibernate for the winter, and it is the smell of
their bodies in the landscape, rubbed on balsam firs as they
passed, grease in the sand and rocks, that is their undoing; it
brings the hunting dogs and the brothers-in-law. In one version
of the tale, told by Jake Jackson, an Inland Tlingit, there is a
moment when the girl, pregnant with the bear's child, plans her
betrayal with all the potent drama of a Russian novel:

After a while, when she is going to feel the snow outside, first she feels her husband all around his body like she is loving him. She hugged her husband and stroked his hair all over.

Then she moved outdoors and felt the snow. Then it's soft. She makes a big snowball with her hands, and she knows the snowball will slide down. She knows that the den is high above a snowslide. She throws the ball down to the bottom of the hill to the creek.

The girl has four brothers staying at the mouth of the river. (McC 18)

The tender attention paid by the wife to her husband's body, the detailed steps of her betrayal, and the subtle note of portent, all serve to heighten the drama. It comes as no surprise that the youngest brother discovers the snowball some months later and follows the track of it with his dogs who have smelled something both familiar and dangerous and run barking to the den.

Gary Snyder looks at a Tlingit version of this story in his essay, "The Woman Who Married a Bear", and tells us that the young woman who marries the bear and then tries to come back to her human family has been too altered by her experience with the Bear Husband to go on as a human. At first she is isolated by her people, given a separate camp in order to gradually re-enter the life of her village. Much is made of the fact that she will need new clothing in order to return. In Maria John's splendid version, the girl tells her brothers, " . . . tell mother to sew a dress for me so I can go home. Sew a dress for the girl, and pants and a shirt for the boy. And moccasins." (McC32) In one Tlingit version, she becomes a bear and kills her brothers. In Tate's version, the woman's children go off to their father's people after an incident with their human grandmother when she doesn't recognize them as her grandchildren. Their mother lets them go: "sorrowful mother was very sorrow." In this version, she is an outsider to both cultures, a taboo-breaker in her own and a betrayer of her grizzly husband among bears. But as well as teaching lessons about proper treatment of a bear's corpse and respect between species, the story reverberates across the cultures, giving form and beauty to the darker secrets of sexuality.

All summer we'd hear our dogs barking, but farther away, probably driving the young bear around the other side of the lake where there was more privacy. I imagined him to be around the mouth of Ruby Creek where it enters Sakinaw Lake, a protected haven of blossoming hardhack, bullrush and thickets of blackberry bushes. It thrilled me to know he was out there, possibly to be encountered on the high trail to Klein Lake — we found scats there, too, and my older son saw him once while mountain-biking — or maybe even up in our berry patch on Mount Hallowell, come August, *the month of wild berries picking*. Once, walking in the woods, my younger son and I smelled the sudden sharp stink of bear and knew that he must've just passed; the dogs shot into the dense bush, bellowing at the tops of their voices.

One of my deepest memories involves a bear rug. It was on a floor next to a fireplace and I remember lying the full length of it, trying to match my body to the bear's. The hairs were glossy black and coarse and I plunged my fingers deep into the coat to get some sense of their texture. The smell was earthy and I remember feeling drowsy in the warm room. A fairy-tale

I loved in those years was "East of the Sun, West of the Moon" and in that story, a girl is sold by her family to a mysterious white bear who carries her to his palatial home deep within a mountain. In the course of the tale, we discover that the bear is a prince who has been bewitched and by her loyalty, courage, and finally love, the young girl frees him from the spell, giving him back his human form and then living with him happily ever after. The directive from the bear that the girl not look at him while he is sleeping echoes other versions of "The Girl Who Married a Bear", notably the versions told to Catherine McClellan by Tommy Peters, an Inland Tlingit:

> And they were making a place to dry fish the way people used to. And finally one morning she pulled off her blanket under which she had been sleeping. It was early in the morning, and she looked at the people there. And there were some people sleeping right across the fire there in one place. Her husband had told her not to ever try to get up in the morning at any time. So when she looked across at the people, she saw that there was nothing but bears lying all around that fire. (McC 24–5);

and the version by Maria Johns, of coastal Tlingit ancestry:

> So they stayed there. When they went to bed, he said, "Don't lift your head in the morning and look at me, even if you wake up before I do." (McC 29)

> (The girl in Maria John's story has yet to discover that the good-looking young man, marked with red paint on his face, who has helped her with her berries and then made a fire for her and cooked gophers is really a bear.)

"East of the Sun, West of the Moon" is a story, one of many, that offered a metaphor for the emerging sexuality of girls, one that went a considerable distance to acknowledge the mysteries inherent in desire. Like "Beauty and the Beast", "Hans My Hedgehog" and "Bearskin", the tale of the young girl taken by the white bear addresses the attraction of adolescent girls to risk and the unknown (I think of this every time I see a teenaged girl hitchiking alone on the highway or else clinging to the back of a black-leather clad, helmeted man on a large motorcycle . . .). This attraction is beautifully articulated in Denise Levertov's poem, "An Embroidery (1)". Two girls, Rose Red and Rose White are preparing a meal for a bear:

> Rose Red's cheeks are burning,
> sign of her ardent, joyful
> compassionate heart.

> Rose White is pale,
> turning away when she hears
> the bear's paw on the latch.

The bear arrives, eats the meal and falls asleep on the hearth while the girls sing to him. Then the two of them get into their feather bed, Rose Red to dream

> . . . she is combing the fur of her cubs
> with a golden comb.

But Rose White can't sleep, possibly because she is aroused by the presence of the bear who represents something more than domestic bliss for her:

Rose White shall marry the bear's brother.
Shall he too
when the time is ripe,
step from the bear's hide?
Is that other, her bridegroom,
here in the room?

The parallels with the Tlingit and Tagish tales are fascinating but for me the most interesting aspect is the fact that
the young girl in "The Girl Who Married the Bear" does not
have her relationship to her bear lover sanitized by a fortuitous
transformation on the part of the bear to the more acceptable
form of a human prince. Rather, the experience with the bear is
the source of her transformation: little by little she grows extra
fur (an allusion to the changes brought by puberty), teeth, her
metabolism adapts so that she is able to sleep for long periods
and wake to eat briefly before sleeping again, and of course
she has been able to conceive children in her relationship with
her bear husband. (A beautiful piece of ivory sculpture from
the Dorset Culture shows a woman taking the penis of a bear
into herself. As impossible as the union sounds, the sculpture
makes it seem entirely natural.) Unfortunately for her husband,
the girl's transformation is not complete enough and she allows
him to be sacrificed so that she can return to her human family.
Yet the old adage is true, you can't go home and expect life to
continue as though nothing had happened. In some versions of
the story, she dons a grizzly bear cloak that her brothers have
asked her to wear so that they can practise their hunting skills.
She warns them that she doesn't want to wear the cloak but they
insist and her mother coaxes her to go along with their request.
She knows that if she wears the cloak, she will become a bear for

once and for all. They insist and so she wears the cloak and kills her human brothers, running off afterwards in the direction of the bear dens, sometimes with her cubs and sometimes leaving them in the human camp. She is the one who is changed beyond imagination or perhaps by imagination.

The bear in our woods only ever came up by the house once, early on an October morning; we heard a commotion outside, heard the dogs barking wildly right by the house, and then gradually getting farther away. When we got up, we found that our compost heap had been torn apart, the enclosure where we keep our garbage cans ripped apart and one can emptied on the driveway, and muddy bear-paw prints on the back trunk of our small car where I'd left a sack of dog food the day before, intending (then forgetting) to bring it into the house. And looking closely, we could see that he'd actually bit through the bumper of the car, trying to get into the trunk. The breadth of his jaw was formidable. He was confident enough, even tailed by dogs, to leave a huge pile of dark purple scat, flecked with the seeds of ripe salal and blackberry, beside the garden. No one walked on it, no one tread over it, even by accident, and the pile stayed until the big rains of November washed it away. And these December days, when we walk by the marshy area to see the carcasses of sockeye washed up on the shore of Sakinaw Lake, I keep my eyes and ears open for him.

Recently I dreamed of the bear-skin rug, brought up out of deep memory for this thinking about bears. In the dream I was stretched out on the rug as I was as a child, arms reaching up the shoulders of the skin as though I was being carried on a journey, willingly, by the fine body that once wore this skin. I was no longer a child, though, but the woman I am now, middle-aged, mother of children, one a daughter on the very edge of puberty. And it came as no surprise to me as I dreamed of the bear-skin, that it turned to me, not a pelt removed from its proud owner, but the bear himself, beautiful and whole, turning to me to embrace me. What I felt was not desire, exactly, but recognition, that here was the natural consequence of riding the bear-skin in imagination, here was the return of the lord of the forest. And I was willing to go with him.

In a way, what the story confirms is that fertility and desire are to some extent beyond our reason; sexuality is an ancient conundrum, a riddle, something far more mysterious than the human construct our age, poised at the threshold of the millennium, has us believe it to be. Beyond our reason, mammals exist, aware of one another across the boundaries of species and propriety. When I crouch in the woods to pee on our walks, my dogs (two spayed females) wait for me to rise before pausing and peeing in the same place. And I sometimes wonder, seeing their noses at work in the air, what it is that lets them know a bear is near. Does a thread of danger pass through the air like spider silk or something richer and enigmatic, the smell of power? In the Parks Canada directive to seal tampons in an airtight plastic bag, what is left unspoken is whether the bears would come because of the odour of blood, anyone's blood, or because they knew that fertile women were among the group. "If a bear rears up on its hind legs and waves its nose in the air, it is trying to identify you." And how will it know? By smell again, or by the exposing of one's genitals: "My husband, it's me . . . "?

What the story of "The Girl Who Married a Bear" tells us is complicated and original, that for those of us who live in their territory, the bears are integral to our lives in the way that the plants are, and the birds, the snakes sunning themselves in the warm grass, that we must learn to read the signs of their passing and pay attention to the messages therein. It is no wonder that people have worshipped bears as symbols of fecundity, as a Goddess in some incarnations and as a bridegroom in others. We can see the piles of bear excrement in a number of ways. The seeds and grasses, fish eggs and insects contained within are microcosms of the world, the very stuff of creation. And perhaps most fascinating in terms of femininity and risk, the piles are a warning, that we have entered bear country and must mind our step; and they are an invitation, not to be taken lightly, to enter the world of the bear's embrace.

> . . . It's before young man reached the place to where the den was, that Black-Bear teached his Princess how to sing as soon as he die, and when he cut, it will sing again, and when they dried his skin the other song and at roast the Bear's heart another song, and when the skin was dried then put the red-ore at back from head to tail, and put also red-ore across under arms. Thus the Bear have said to his wife the Princess, and they shall put my skin at the side of a fire to dried it. When you hear a little crake noise, then you shall know that I am chilly and you shall make more fire. Thus said the Bear to her. (Tate 38)

Postscript in May, 1997

IT'S NEARING THE long weekend when my daughter will join girls of her age to ride on a parade float as queens and princesses of May in our community. For this they need dresses, or gowns really, and a willing group of mothers to help plan and decorate the float.

My daughter's gown is finished, a blue so true to nature that I keep seeing it around me — in the opening buds of pulmonaria and scilla, the intense spring sky, the carpet of a flower I'm not familiar with over in an abandoned homestead by Sakinaw Lake where we go to collect long lengths of ivy to garland the sides of the flatbed truck that the mothers are transforming into a spring grove for their daughters.

The bear has been around again this spring. We haven't seen him yet although the dogs have been barking and running into the woods in the early mornings and we've seen the piles of excrement on our walks for the past two weeks. I've been studying them, wondering at the diet of the bear, how he can sustain himself on grasses and what appear to be shoots of thimbleberry and primeval horsetails. Wondering too, when I find piles on the trail that is one of our property boundaries, whether he was entering our woods or leaving them when he left his mark.

Depending on whether you think of May as early spring or late spring turning to early summer, this is *the month of seals' cubs* or *the month of eggs* in the Tsimshian calendar. I've been watching the violet-green swallows courting for the last month and taking dry grass into the little house they return to year after year by the vegetable garden. And there have been shards of pale mossy shell or speckled grey fragments on the trail, possibly as a result of the ravens' nest-robbing that I know is taking place because I hear the ravens all day long, plotting and scheming in the tall cedars. And my daughter, nearly twelve, is in full bloom, her small breasts filling out the bodice of the blue gown, and her moods changeable as the moon.

On the eve of the last day before the final decorating bee, she comes with me to the tangled garden on the creek feeding into Sakinaw Lake. We've gone to the creek in the fall with a biologist friend who monitors a small coho run and nearby there's a sockeye run, the rosy fish spawning in gravel about six feet off the shore of the lake. We know the bears come for the fish then because we find the carcasses pulled up into tall grass and we've seen the eagles waiting in the trees. I find myself wondering if the bears keep the memory of these succulent fish in their minds all summer, waiting and feeding on greens, grubs, even crayfish that I've seen in the creeks, but all the while longing for salmon flesh and the tender eggs. And is it memory that takes them up the mountain on late summer mornings for ripe blackberries, memory that brings them to the strong fence around our orchard where trees of pears and apples sit in the grass like maidens?

My daughter swims while I pull ivy down out of the trees. She amuses herself by holding her feet very still until bullheads come to nibble at her ankles. Then she wraps herself in a towel and comes to find me. We probably have enough ivy but I want to cut some extra now rather than having to come back for it if more is necessary. We make our way carefully through the periwinkle, a little wild patch of lilies of the valley, and some vicious canes of blackberry.

"O look," says my daughter, pointing, and there is a fresh pile of bear dung, right in the path we are travelling, a place we have come to before, looking for clumps of daylilies and poppies gone wild. She knows the story of the girl who married the bear and she knows about the necessity of minding one's way, about the dangers and pleasures of encountering animals in these coastal woods.

"He's been eating grass," I tell her. "See how the stools are threaded with it. You can even see the seeds."

All around us the wild grasses are growing, heavy with seeds not yet ripened. The sound of the water is lovely, running to the lake, tiny smolts making their way down to it and eventually across it to the ocean. The sun is setting over the hump of Nelson Island and the woods are getting darker. It doesn't feel like it did half an hour ago, before we found the pile of dung, shafts of light coming through the spaces between maples and conifers and filtered sun dappling the ground.

"Time to go," I tell my daughter, "and stay with me, please."

We fill our arms with ivy, draping the long vines of it over our shoulders, and walk to the truck parked over by the boat ramp. I am holding her hand. Birds are singing so beautifully and the noise of the creek is so loud with snow melt and weeks of rain that we say nothing as we leave.

❧

WELL

WE'D MET UP in Dublin, my son Forrest coming directly from university in Toronto and I from British Columbia. It was May of 2001, the same month I'd first arrived in Ireland twenty-three years earlier. It was something of a sentimental journey for me and a discovery for my son, as we hoped to explore Connemara where I'd once lived. After a few days in Dublin, we went by train to Galway where we had planned to rent a car for a week.

The rental did not go smoothly. I had somehow expected that we would arrive at the train station, quickly procure the car and be on our way west within an hour. We hadn't counted on a shifty fellow claiming to have the only rental vehicle left in the city; and we eventually signed forms for enough complicated insurance we might have rented the Holy Grail. We felt insulted rather than blessed, were given the keys, and we walked to a side lane off Eyre Square where a small dirty Nissan Micra waited in a cloud of old tobacco smoke, inside and out.

So long since I'd driven on the left side of the road, so long since I'd needed to find my way along narrow streets marked with signs that no longer made sense. "Traffic Calming" one announced, but instead of soporific lines of cars, there was a concrete abutment in the middle of the road which I had to ease the Micra around, contrary to instinct and reflex, while other motorists honked and tailgated. Heaven help a driver new to Irish motorways. But then a sign did make sense, Clifden Road Ahead. It was the road to my past, and my heart tugged a little as we made the turn.

A few kilometres out of Galway, we were driving through the rocky landscape I had come to find. The dark lakes, gorse coming into bloom, and the smell of turf smoke so sweetly unexpected that I stopped on the shoulder of the road, away from traffic, so we could breath it in. Oughterard with the tree-hung river and small hotels, signs leading to Lough Corrib and its ancient crannogs, cottages in fields beyond the road with that low familiar shape . . .

I'd forgotten about the sheep, but soon we had to slow for them, black-faced, white fleeces streaked with blue or red, raddle marks left by rams to indicate successful servicing. (The rams wear a harness around their chests holding a chalky crayon which marks the ewes they have tupped.) The sheep appeared out of nowhere, at ease on pavement as they surveyed the horizon. On delicate feet they tripped from the road when cars approached, the young ones uttering their plaintive bleats. Twigs of gorse and golden grass trailed from their fleeces.

I'd forgotten the way a heart stops when the road drops down in Clifden. Half a lifetime and so little had changed: the same streets wrapped around the central shops and pubs, the bank, the newsagents on the corner, the sound of the river racing beyond Bridge Street. Our room was waiting — window flung open onto a little garden, pink washed walls, faded quilts, towels smelling of fresh air.

I wanted to eat on the strand opposite the island where I'd lived and we found the grocery store where it had always been, though it was now larger, and had a deli; we bought cold chicken, bread, tomatoes and apples, and drove out the Sky Road. I missed the turn-off, which I had taken so many times in my past, on foot or borrowed bicycle, laden with provisions, books from the library to last out the storms and weeks of bad weather. But there was a group of new houses at the corner and nothing looked quite as it had, until we backtracked, turned, and found ourselves on the narrow road leading to the beach past Miceal O'Gorham's house in its grove of wind-bent conifers. A dog mournfully watched us pass. We had to stop while John Smith drove his cattle to their evening pasture, him still in the black wellingtons with a familiar dog at the heels of the last wild-eyed heifer. He waved as though to anyone and for a moment I thought to call to him, asking him . . . but what? Where have the years gone, John Smith, that you are still with the cattle and I am driving with a son the age I was when I lived on the island we'll see when we park the car and take our picnic to the sand.

We had the *Ordnance Survey Map Discovery Series 37*. It showed numerous sites which I had walked by twenty years ago without knowing they existed. A holy well for instance, in Miceal O'Gorham's very field, fenced in rusted wire and woody fuchsia, a sign now asking that no one enter because of Foot and Mouth Disease. I half-wanted to knock on Miceal's door to say, Do you remember me and might we walk on your field? but something kept me from doing so. He had been a romantic figure to encounter on the road, a man with property, a wild Heathcliff profile, an ailing mother kept in a room off the kitchen. A handsome man, cagey in his dealings with cattle and horses, with a reputation for violence, a way of looking at women which disarmed them and I suspect disrobed one or two. So we walked up a hill opposite instead where, by following the contours of the map which remarkably matched the way the hill rose, we found a megalithic tomb facing away from the sea. Wind blew and birds trilled, and we sat on the rocks in front of the tomb where inside lay the bones of someone buried four thousand years earlier, a hip pierced with an arrow-tip, a pin dropped from a cloak long since disintegrated lying alongside. I lost my shoe in the bog as we returned to the car, and everywhere there was bog bean, marsh marigolds, the finished blooms of lady's smock. When I woke the next morning, I knew immediately where I was, the sound of the town waking as familiar as my own household. My remaining muddy shoe, rinsed in the little sink in our bathroom, hung out the window. Desmond, with a tea-towel wrapped about his middle, brought us our breakfast and a steaming silver-plated coffee pot. Fine weather was promised, kind words exchanged.

∾

On Omey Island, accompanied by a saint . . .

We took our ordnance map of the west of Ireland, our water bottles, our notebooks, our guides to birds and flowers, and walked across the sands to Omey Island, where the nineteenth-century population of 400 has shrunk to fewer than twenty, and ruined houses caught the wind in their chimneys. From the steps of one such house, and perhaps not abandoned after all, a sheep dog ran joyfully to meet us. There were burrs in its coat and when it rolled over on the lane, wiggling in ecstasy to have its belly rubbed, we could tell that it was a male. We walked for a mile or so, seeing no one but a man unloading lobster pots from the boot of an old car, and then we made our way up to the headland. A path was indicated on the map but we saw no path, nor the middens also noted on the map, just an expanse of green grass and pale sand. The dog kept running ahead, returning to us in delight, then bounding off to burrow half his body in an entrance to the rabbit warrens we could see evidence of in the dunes. We saw small piles of rabbit droppings. And there were quick elegant bodies slipping into the earth, never quite where the dog pursued them. There were daisies and primroses, sand-spurry and sea-blush. Years ago, when I lived on an island south of Omey, I had come by boat to see the first signs of a chapel emerging from the sand. Those who brought me were not surprised that a chapel might rise from the sand or a small field of graves reveal themselves.

No one mentioned the well on that earlier visit. Or had they and I'd simply forgotten? A young woman does not necessarily connect with stories she hears told quietly, containing within them old habits or superstitions. I knew the chapel had been named for St. Feichin and was not surprised to read somewhere that the well was named for him too. It was located near the shore, a long stone-lined passage leading from it to the high-tide line. Tides would fill the stone enclosure at certain times of the year. We were surprised to see photographs and letters tucked into zip-locked bags, and many coins and tiny articles of clothing fastened to the stones around the well. Some egg-shaped rocks rested on the edge. There were plenty of those on the shore and I picked up a particularly pretty white one, made a vague wish about future prosperity, and ceremoniously placed the rock on the lip of the well. Forrest and I each dropped a Canadian quarter into the water, too.

We walked on with our canine guide to the fifteenth-century chapel, a beautiful structure of pink granite contained within a bowl of collapsed dune, circumscribed by the remains of a stone wall. So long since worshippers came to sit under its roof to praise God, some of them since buried on the headland. There was an area called Cnocán na mBan, the hill of the women, a remnant of the old antipathy to women implicit in St. Feichin's hagiography, although he was not alone among the male saints in his attitudes. The presence of women in a church or in a cemetery, even after death, was unthinkable to those bleak ascetics. In the newer graveyard, built on top of another older one, crosses claimed their dead while wildflowers covered old earth and new earth. I said I would rather be buried among women on the headland, facing north-west, with rabbits burrowing among the daisies, but truth is the dunes collapse and build up, no place is what it seems, permanent or temporary. Things materialize from the sand upon occasion — a tool, a hasp, a leg-bone from someone long gone to God, pottery from local clay.

The dog disappeared before we began our walk across the strand to the car (Omey Island is tidal and accessible on foot except during the year's highest tides). One moment he was happily stretching out to have his belly tickled and the next he had vanished into the clear air of the day. I'd like to have thanked him for such excellent company and for alerting us to rabbits.

Returning to Clifden, we went to the library to look things up — flowers pressed into my notebook, a bird, information about the church and the ancient parish of Omey. The librarian was happy to sign us up as members so we could use the computer to check our email and take books along with us on subsequent jaunts. Idly running my fingers along the spines of the volumes on one shelf, I noticed a book on holy wells. Delighted, I took it to one of the big chairs and curled up to read. Was St. Feichin's well included? It was. The text described it as a fertility well, mentioned the egg-shaped rocks and noted that women hoping to become pregnant placed them by the well. I showed the entry to Forrest and we exchanged looks of mutual horror. I quietly returned the book to its shelf.

ॐ

Slow is every foot upon an unknown path.
(Irish proverb)

We were coming back from Killary Harbour, and Forrest noticed a number of things on the map which we could see by taking a third class road leaving the Westport road near Moyard. I stopped the car on the side of the main road because we couldn't really see any roads where the map said one should be. Ah, we discovered, reading the legend — there are two kinds of third class roads: the ones wider than four meters and the ones narrower. This was one of the narrower ones so maybe it was that opening in the trees. And we turned.

After a short distance on gravel and grass, we came to a farmyard. The road appeared to go through the middle of it. Chickens were pecking at the ground and a black and white sheepdog watched us approach. Two men were talking in sunlight, dressed in suits, one with a tie and wearing a lapel pin of the Pioneer Total Abstinence Association of the Sacred Heart. I stopped the car and rolled down the window.

"Excuse me, we have a map which shows a road . . . "

They looked at each other and then at us. A few words were spoken between them. I got out of the car with the map.

"Is it a map ye have then?" Both of them came towards us as though I was carrying the relics of a saint.

"Just here, you see, it shows a road. Is this it?"

One of the men, the one not wearing a tie, proved to have an extreme speech impediment but he was very eager. I think he told us that we were parked in his farm yard, that the chickens were his, as were the fields we could see. The other man, seeing my confusion, came forward to act as a translator.

"It is his land, to be sure. A road, is it? Ye're wanting a road?" It seemed to baffle both men that someone might want to drive on a road that appeared on a map and which passed through a peaceful yard, geraniums in tubs by the door and a pile of straw outside a shed.

"We are trying to find some standing stones that are shown on the map. They look like they'd be in the open, near here. Do you know them?"

They exchanged words again with each other and the man with the tie said, "There is a stone, yes, in a field just down the road here. If ye stop and look over the neighbour's wall, ye'll see it in the field with the sheep so."

"So this is the road we take?"

"It is, it is. It is very narrow and ye must drive slowly." He was translating his friend's concern that we would not be able to see if another car was coming but from the look of the road, no car had been on it for a long time. Primroses grew in the grassy patches between the gravel.

'Ye're not Irish, aren ye?'

"No, we're from Canada." This elicted great delight, both of them reaching out to clasp my hands between their own, much nodding and smiling.

"And ye'll be careful to drive slowly so?"

"O, yes, I'll be careful. I've been driving for thirty years without an accident."

"Thirty years! Never! Ye canna be that old to be driving so long so."

"This is my son," I said proudly. As though to prove my age, my tall son smiled from the passenger seat.

"Ah, he's never yer son! Well, ye've the gift of youth on ye anyway. God bless."

With that, we were on our way, nosing the little car between blossoming hawthorne which reached into the windows to tickle our noses with its sweet smell. It formed a dense hedge, with fuchsia among it, on either side of the narrow road and the raised banks white with wild garlic, yellow with primroses. Birds sang unseen within its depths.

A small cottage lay ahead among hawthorns, fenced with stone, curtains twitching at the windows, and beyond it we saw the standing stone, on a sloping field above Ballynakill Harbour. There were sheep grazing around it, tufts of their fleece caught on the lichens growing over its surface.

A stone planted in a field by people wanting to mark an occasion — a death? the passage of the sun at a memorable point in the year? a place of intense energy? I had seen Stonehenge, tried to take its measure among the tour groups and kiosks but this was different. The stone was calm in its history, useful to sheep, perhaps aligned with others in the vicinity, although the point is often made that most have vanished into the landscape, used for buildings, roadbeds. So this stone was monumental in its very ordinariness. No wonder the men had to think before they could tell us where to find this thing indicated on our map, marked as history, but unheralded in a neighbour's field. And the road which they never would have thought important enough for anyone other than a man driving his cattle from one pasture to the next, the postman on his bicycle, a woman gathering wild garlic for spring flavour, a road defined by hedges stitched together with bluebells and bloody cranesbill. A map is a transparency, a set of codes, which might not make much sense to someone living deeply in its contours without knowing those codes are anything special.

We were annotating our map as we went along, noting the date we passed a place or visited a ruin. It would add our layer of experience to the formal layers already present — the cartographers' work, the duplicity of names, the overlay of colonization and transgressions of one sort or another.

"What shall I write on the map?" asked Forrest.

"Put down *the magic road*, and the date," I replied.

And there was more. At the end of the road, we could see from the map there was a holy well. It was difficult to find: the road shown was not a road but a track, unused (or so it seemed), winding behind a cottage with the requisite dog watching curiously as we drove up a gravelly slope. We found a length of pipe coming out of a bank and we were prepared to be impressed, thinking it a contemporary gloss or practical modification. But then we saw the true well. One book told us that "a holy well can be defined simply as any location where water is used as the focal point of supernatural divination, cure or devotion . . . " We had also learned that many of them carried a history far older than the Christian implications in their names, their associations with saints. Long before people came to them for the diseases connected with the specific saint — eye problems, warts, mental illness, festering sores, infertility (although I was trying to forget I had made a wish at a well used for just such a condition I did wonder why a saint who kept women from his structures should be somehow sympathetic to difficulties a woman might have in conceiving a child) — , the wells had been important sites for ritual in earlier times. Sacred, powerful, the waters inspired rituals which lingered long after the advent of Christianity. In recognition of this, many sites were appropriated by the Church, given a patron saint, the new sanctity building on the old. We have a well at home, the source for our household's water, but it is drilled deep into bedrock, partly cased in iron; the water is pumped into our house through pvc pipe. I began to think a little more about water, though, and the way it comes from the earth, the way we notice it and use it, the miracles we attribute to it. Later on we saw other wells that were simply depressions in rock with water coming from an unknown source, green with cress, and perhaps housed in a nineteenth-century hut. A trail would tell us people had been coming forever.

The true well at the end of the magic road somehow fit our expectations, though we weren't aware of having had them. It was enclosed by a circular stone wall, waist-high, with mossy steps leading down to the pool, and was filled with clear water. When we threw in our coins, they vanished, which told us it was deep. There were photographs stuck to the stone wall, packages with letters, coins, tatters of cloth. Ivy climbed over the stones and other plants — toadflax, herb robert, wild strawberries, primroses — grew in a splendid profusion. We could hear nothing but birds, peace hanging in the air like a curtain. So it was a surprise later to discover that the well's patron saint, Ceannanach, beheaded somewhere near Cleggan (the nearest village) by a pagan chief, had carried his head to the source and washed it, replacing it on his neck before lying down to die by the pure water.

Ceannanach's church was nearby. It was hidden in trees overlooking Ballynakill Lough, a place of leafy stillness. Climbing over the stone wall to enter the roofless remains, I looked, as is my usual habit, for snakes in the warm grass and then remembered that of course there are no snakes in Ireland, another saintly miracle, courtesy of Patrick. Only lizards, one kind of toad, frogs (though I've never seen a frog in Ireland). The churchyard seemed a more likely place to hear owls or encounter hedgehogs at dusk but in the afternoon there was nothing but birdsong and midges. Ancient thick walls and decorated stones, bladder campion and violets threaded through the grass. Beautiful the fit of the stones together, the rough openings for windows, with worked lintels and a small amount of decorative detail. You could imagine owls here or the murmur of voices within the walls of the church, perhaps offering the Latin responses, or singing a medieval hymn. And sitting very still we heard voices, not the Belgians who stopped their van and set up painting gear on the side of the road, but the pure notes of praise. *Patricii laudes semper dicamus, May we always speak praise of Patrick, ut nos cum illo defendat Deus, so that through him God will defend us* . . . I almost hated to start the engine of the car to drive away, not wanting to disturb that evensong.

∾

The green field re-echoes, where there is a brisk bright stream . . .
(Irish, ninth-century nature poem)

Passing Ballynakill Lough, we saw the island that the map told us was a crannog or a man-made fortified island, we saw a ring fort on the crest of a hill, more standing stones watching our progress on the unfamiliar path. The weather was perfect for a visit to a beach of white sand, blue water, the graceful company of gulls. We drove to Sellerna Bay where I had walked to swim years ago when I lived for a time in Cleggan. I didn't remember a tomb although the map showed one right in a field by the sand's edge and sure enough, when we knew what we were looking for, there it was, a wedge tomb facing the sunset. Primroses grew in the grass around it and a small red flower that I thought must be pimpernel. I tried to imagine what lay beneath its mound, the portal opening left for the soul to escape or for food to be presented in some mysterious ritual to nourish or placate the dead. Excavations of tombs of this period have revealed pottery vessels and tools. I closed my eyes to warm wind and the scent

of grass and thought about the lives of those leaving their
dead in this place. Such rocky ground! What would those early
inhabitants have eaten? Plant pollens tell us something of their
cereal crops and of course there would have been meat. Four
thousand years ago, there were bears in Ireland, wild deer (as
there still are), wolves and sheep. The middens contain shells and
bones, burned stones telling us the shellfish was cooked. When I
lived here in 1978, I had almost no money and gathered mussels
and nettles for my soup-pot, pried the meat out of winkles with
a pin. Sometimes I would be given a crab or mackerel to cook.
But often I grazed fields like this one, searching for silverweed,
wild garlic, cress in the damp corners. Later we learned that
the patterns of stones in this field were not random but were
the remains of Bronze age field boundaries. A landscape is so
literal — it is what it is, made of what is there, yet there is a sense
of textual meaning once the materials can be decoded and read.
How many places are there on the planet untouched by farmers,
ancient or modern, how many seas never fished by nets, how
many mountains unclimbed by conquering feet? And what does
a field boundary do to our apprehension of history, of place?
Once noted, it cannot be forgotten and a wild field at the edge
of the Atlantic takes on a gloss of use and husbandry.

The map promised something called a cillín. I knew that cill
or kill meant church so we walked to the end of the sand, looking
for the remains of a church. On the map, the site appeared to be
along the shore of a creek leading into Sellerna Bay. We found
the creek but nothing else, just rocks and primroses and shells
left by gulls. It was a lovely location, in sunlight, overlooked
by some farms, the creek very swift and clean. But something
of a mystery. Later, in County Kerry, following another map,

we tried to find a cillín and couldn't so I asked in the library if the woman at the desk spoke Irish. She did. I explained that we had been trying to find cillíns indicated on maps and there seemed to be nothing there and were we looking for churches or something else? She was not friendly at all and said she didn't know, churches probably, but she was obviously not interested in helping us find out. It wasn't until months later, when my son came home for Christmas, bringing with him a copy of the *Archaeological Inventory of West Galway*, did I learn that a cillín was a children's burial ground. They were accorded their own section in the Inventory and "are characterised by the presence of numerous small, uninscribed set stones, often arranged in rows." Would we have recognized the place for what it was had we known it was a burial ground not just for children but for others "perceived to be in some way outside of society: aborted foetuses, strangers, suicides and Famine victims . . . "? (A child conceived because of a wish at the well of St. Feichin and then a husband or lover disappearing or failing to materialize in the first place after love beneath flowering trees?) And was the librarian somehow reluctant to share with us the added association with Limbo and "otherness"? I knew from living for a year on a remote Irish island how a person could be called a blow-in, never mind the length of their residence, and never accommodated, alive, in the usual way. How lonely for a child or a stranger to be buried so far from a church, a home, left only an uninscribed stone which a person, a stranger herself, coming later could not even recognize. And yet there was water nearby, that bright creek and the open sea, hooded crows among the cow pats and snow buntings in winter at the high tide mark, the occasional woman gathering seaweed for her potatoes. Maybe on a quiet day, the voices from distant churches might be carried to the sad stones: *In memoria eterna erit iustus, the just one will be in eternal memory . . . Hibernenses omnes clamant ad te pueri, the children of Ireland cry out to thee . . .* And who of us knows what company might be there when life leaves us, alone or not, birds rising from the field light as souls?

∾

Do Not Enter. Area Closed Due to Foot and Mouth Disease
(sign seen all over Ireland, 2001)

We didn't see St. Patrick's Well off the Maam Valley road, nor his Bed a little further on. We drove as far as the path to that Well but then it led through a farm yard and the sign told us Do Not Enter. Later in our trip, we ignored the signs and ventured into Hoare Abbey, a field of beehive huts on the Dingle Peninsula, a grove of ogham stones on a private drive, but we hadn't yet found the courage to climb the gate, and walk up the path smoothed by centuries of travellers and believers.

We didn't see a tomb off the Streamstown road for the same reason, nor the promontory fort off the Lower Road. We did walk down to Clifden Castle past standing stones which later proved to be follies, according to the *Archaeological Inventory of West Galway*; we read this with chagrin, remembering our attempts to determine something from the way the stones were aligned on their slope leading down towards the sea. But fake as they might be in their current placement, I thought the stones themselves could have been brought to the castle grounds from somewhere nearby where they'd stood since the dawn of time.

We found the broken bodies of infant rooks fallen from the nests all along the towers, while the walls resounded with the echoes of those who had not fallen but grown to noisy maturity. Nettles brushed our legs in the shrubbery and cattle scattered from the rooms of the ruined castle. All of this could be explained by evolution, nettles replacing ornate plantings, the cattle kept by local farmers who had procured the lands previously held by the Eyre estate (themselves tenants for generations), the corpses of the birds a warning to those free spirits leaning too far from the safety of the nest.

We didn't see the signal tower beyond Cleggan Farm or the cairn on Tully Mountain — those signs again. We walked in the direction of the Mass Rock beyond Glencraff but didn't get that far, nor did we take the ferry to Inishbofin to see the star-shaped fort, or the fort of Grace O'Malley, although I had gone there as a young woman, so wrapped up in my fierce longing for a fisherman's love that I walked the quiet roads of the island without seeing anything but my own sorrow translated to ruined walls, the corpse of a seal on the rocks.

But we heard owls in the trees around St. Mary's Chapel in Clifden when we were walking back from Church Street with a pizza; we heard a myriad of birds on the Roundstone Bog when we walked out to photograph a working, someone's turf spade left against a trench; we found another hidden church on the Cleggan Road by walking into a dense thicket of hawthornes; we saw the emptied face of a lamb on the high trail to the well at Maol Roc, the eyes nipped out but the nose, lips and dark skin intact, and no fleece, no bones anywhere around; and we walked back to Kylemore through a tunnel of wild purple rhododendrons. We sat on a bench at sunset in front of

Kings Bar, drinking a pint of beer, with the voices of children vanishing in the evening, and we saw a girl walking back from the Sky Road with a book in one hand; I recognized the look of ardour on her shining face.

And I wanted my wish at St. Feichin's well to have been worthwhile, though not for fertility — I had three children, the youngest sixteen, and didn't see myself pushing a pram down the country road where I live, as I approached fifty — but perhaps these things are metaphorical. I wished for prosperity which could be fecundity of mind and spirit, riches of the heart. The saint sounds as if he was a resourceful man, converting a pagan sea captain to Christianity and building a monastery and cloister (the chapel came later in his name). Stories about him include the usual details of lepers and sores and obviously he was nervous about women, thinking they needed to be kept separate even after death. And then there was Ceannanach, carefully carrying his head to his well so he could wash it and place it again upon his shoulders before dying.

∾

The longest road out is the shortest road home.
(Irish proverb)

On our last day in Clifden, we packed our cases into the grim car along with our stones, our shells, the books we'd bought, and our water bottles and maps. The owners of the guesthouse, Desmond and Eileen, hugged us away like family, calling *God speed* as we drove off. I had forgotten how heavy is departure, the weight of longing approximate to granite. I'd slept that week in the sultry air of Connemara and did not dream of anything memorable but woke each morning hungry for Eileen's brown bread and an egg carried to the table on a china saucer like a rare jewel.

We were heading south, to County Kerry, and then to Cashel to see Cormac's Chapel on its famous rock. We had no detailed Ordnance Maps to use for that part of the journey, having exhausted our desire to trace the intricate patterns of history across a landscape. We were simply going to look at things which appeared before us — Kilmalkedar Church and the alphabet stone in its churchyard, Gallarus Oratory, Yeat's tower standing above a leafy river. Of course there were more maps, simple ones, for how could there not be with a mother driving a rented car on unfamiliar motorways, a history student for a son, but I did not feel the tug of connection as I did that day on Omey Island with the bones of the women on the bare headland for company, did not hear the voices quietly singing their responses in Ceannanach's church. It was enough for me to watch things pass.

We hadn't come to see only wells, but our map was annotated with their names. At home we have a well, nothing as pretty as Ceannanach's in its veil of ivy, but a source for our household, clean and cold, capped in red iron. In thinking about our search for ruins in the west of Ireland, I was filled with a desire to look at our own local maps and the leftovers of names, what they meant. We were discovering how little a map could tell of a place, and how much, naming and usage at odds with each other or else providing a cryptic commentary on history. Ancient stones, churches, graveyards of children and strangers, wells used to cure boils and infertility — some of these areas protected, some forbidden to women, some lost to immediate memory (those dolmens subsumed in walls, barns . . .), some of them still off-limits because of a new pestilence. It came as no surprise, driving up out of Clifden that day, but thinking of home, to remember the source of our own water. We live in the shadow of Mount Hallowell, named for Captain Hallowell of the HMS Swiftsure, Battle of the Nile. Our well collects water from underground streams running down off Hallowell, a name reaching back into the shadows of our language, giving credence to the notion that behind every name, there is a layer, and another layer, until a ship's captain who never knew our mountain consecrates our water.

Acknowledgements and Notes

Versions of some of these essays have appeared in *Brick*, *Geist*, the online journals *Terrain* and *Wild Thoughts*, *Manoa*, *The Wayward Coast*, *The Puritan*, and *Brindle and Glass Magazine*. "month of wild berries picking" was also published as a chapbook by High Ground Press.

"month of wild berries picking" is a meditation on the nature of stories and their influence in our lives. I am indebted to Julie Cruikshank for her gracious permission to quote from *The Stolen Women: Female Journeys in Tagish and Tutchone* (Ottawa: National Museum of Man Mercury Series: Canadian Ethnology Service Paper No.87, 1983). I would like to thank the Canadian Museum of Civilization for permission to use material from Catharine McClellan's *The Girl Who Married A Bear* (Ottawa: National Museums of Canada, Publications in Ethnology, No.2, 1970). Thanks are also due to Ralph Maude and Columbia University for permission to use material from *The Porcupine Hunter and Other Stories: The Original Tsimshian Texts of Henry Tate* (Vancouver:Talonbooks, 1993); the original texts are located in X898C442 T18, Henry W. Tate manuscripts, Rare Book and Manuscript Library, Columbia University. I am also grateful to New Directions Publishing Corp. for permission to quote from "An Embroidery (1)" by Denise Levertov, from *Poems 1968-1972*, ©1970 by Denise Levertov. Reprinted with permission of New Directions Publishing Corp.

"Erasing the Maps" is for Barbara Lambert, who suggested the title.

"Slow Food" was written in April 2006. A return visit to Powell River in March 2007 had us anticipating lunch at the Kitchen Table. We discovered a new owner and a new name, Bemused, and an excellent lunch in the slow-food tradition (duck sausage with polenta and a salad of miner's lettuce with Saltspring Island goat cheese).

I was blessed with the intelligent and congenial editorial guidance of Harriet Richards for this book.

Thanks to my son Forrest Pass for accompanying me on a wonderful trip to Ireland which occasioned the essay, "Well"; for helping me with endless research questions, all of the magpie variety; and for translating the medieval Latin hymn to St. Patrick which appears in the essay.

Thanks are also due to my son Brendan Pass for his easy and generous mathematical knowledge and his willingness to believe that I *could* learn calculus with a little effort. And I am grateful to my daughter Angelica Pass for her good-natured tolerance of maternal intrusions and for her translation of the lines from Sappho, which I've used as an epigraph for this collection of essays.

Thanks to my husband John Pass for everything.

This book is for my family, immediate and extended, and for my friends. *The more I think about it, the more I realize how little I know about the weight of love.*

Works Cited in "month of wild berries picking"

Cruikshank, Julie. *The Stolen Women: Female Journeys in Tagish and Tutchone.* National Museum of Man Mercury Series, Canadian Ethnology Service Paper No. 87. Ottawa: National Museums of Canada, 1983.

Hague, Kathleen & Michael. *East of the Sun and West of the Moon.* New York: Harcourt Brace Jovanovich, 1980.

Levertov, Denise. *Relearning the Alphabet.* New York: New Directions Books, 1970.

McClellan, Catherine. *The Girl Who Married The Bear: A Masterpiece of Indian Oral Tradition.* National Museum of Man, Publications in Ethnology, No. 2. Ottawa: National Museums of Canada, 1970.

Rockwell, David. *Giving Voice to Bear: North American Indian Myths, Rituals, and Images of the Bear.* New York: Roberts Rinehart Publishers, 1991.

Snyder, Gary. *The Practise of the Wild.* San Francisco: North Point Press, 1990.

Tate, Henry. Maud, Ralph, ed. *The Porcupine Hunter and Other Stories: The Original Tsimshian Texts of Henry Tate.* Vancouver: Talonbooks, 1993.

Teit, James. *The Lillooet Indians.* The Jesup North Pacific Expedition, ed. Franz Boas. Memoir of the American Museum of Natural History. New York: G.E. Stechert, 1906.

THERESA KISHKAN lives with her family on B.C.'s
Sechelt Peninsula. An accomplished poet and essayist,
her work has been anthologized and published widely.
She is the author of six books of poetry, including *Black
Cup*; an anthology of essays, *Red Laredo Boots*; and two
novels, *Sisters of Grass* and *A Man In A Distant Field*.
She operates High Ground Press with her husband
John Pass.